In the aftermath of the World Trade Center attacks, treatment for fear of flying has become more difficult, owing to increased security and restricted access to airplanes for persons in need of exposure therapy. Overcoming Fear of Heights *thus fills a tremendous gap for people who suffer from this disabling fear. Antony and Rowa have done a masterful job with this book. In a clear and gentle fashion, these authors walk the reader through the step-by-step process of conducting exposure, including a remarkably useful section on how to troubleshoot the typical problems that arise during this process. The book is peppered with case examples, which help to illustrate how to overcome your fear of heights. A job well-done!*

> —J. Gayle Beck, Ph.D., is professor of psychology and associate chair of the Department of Psychology at the State University of New York, Buffalo. She is past president of the Association for Behavioral and Cognitive Therapies.

Antony and Rowa have written an excellent book for people who are afraid of heights, people who care about people who are afraid of heights, and people who would like to learn how to help people who are afraid of heights. The book provides clear and helpful instructions, based in the science of behaviour change, that are an excellent guide for those who wish to overcome their fears. Research tells us that there is a very effective treatment for the fear of heights, and this book contains the details.

> —Adam Radomsky, Ph.D., is associate professor of psychology at Concordia University in Montreal, QC. His research investigates cognitive and behavioral aspects of fear and anxiety disorders as well as the treatments that are most effective for them.

The fear of heights can disrupt activities that most people take for granted, such as using an escalator, driving across a bridge, and enjoying the view from a balcony. Antony and Rowa have written a highly practical and easy-to-read book that is packed with strategies scientifically proven to help with overcoming this fear. Anyone with a fear of heights will benefit from this advice, as will the people who care about them.

> —Jonathan S. Abramowitz, Ph.D., ABPP, associate professor of clinical psychology and director of the OCD and Anxiety Clinic at the University of North Carolina at Chapel Hill

overcoming
fear of heights

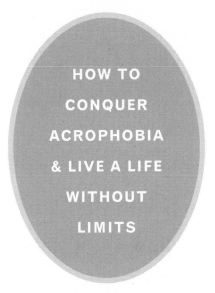

HOW TO
CONQUER
ACROPHOBIA
& LIVE A LIFE
WITHOUT
LIMITS

MARTIN M. ANTONY, PH.D.
KAREN ROWA, PH.D.

New Harbinger Publications, Inc.

Publisher's Note

This publication is designed to provide accurate and authoritative information in regard to the subject matter covered. It is sold with the understanding that the publisher is not engaged in rendering psychological, financial, legal, or other professional services. If expert assistance or counseling is needed, the services of a competent professional should be sought.

Distributed in Canada by Raincoast Books

Copyright © 2007 by Martin M. Antony and Karen Rowa
New Harbinger Publications, Inc.
5674 Shattuck Avenue
Oakland, CA 94609
www.newharbinger.com

Acquired by Catharine Sutker; Cover design by Amy Shoup;
Edited by Brady Kahn; Text design by Tracy Carlson

Library of Congress Cataloging-in-Publication Data

Antony, Martin M.
  : how to conquer acrophobia and live a life without limits / Martin M. Antony and Karen A. Rowa.
    p. cm.
  Includes bibliographical references and index.
  ISBN-13: 978-1-57224-456-6 (alk. paper)
  ISBN-10: 1-57224-456-9 (alk. paper)
  1. Acrophobia--Popular works. I. Rowa, Karen A. II. Title.
  RC552.A43A58 2007
  616.85'225--dc22

                       2007005761

09 08 07

10 9 8 7 6 5 4 3 2 1   First printing

For my stepfather, Ben Ruekberg, who passed away about a week before we finished writing this book, and who introduced me to *High Anxiety*, Mel Brooks's classic film that's all about conquering one's height phobia, among other things.

—MMA

For Audrey.

—KR

"I don't have a fear of heights. I do, however, have a fear of falling from heights."

—George Carlin

Contents

Acknowledgments

We would like to thank the staff at New Harbinger Publications for all of its hard work surrounding this book. Thanks especially to our editors, Catharine Sutker and Brady Kahn, to Amy Shoup for another great cover, to Dorothy Smyk (director of sales), Earlita Chenault (our publicist), and Michele Waters and Tracy Carlson for their work on the production of the book. Thanks also to Drs. Randi McCabe and Mark Watling, who, as coauthors of previous books in this series (on animal phobias and medical phobias, respectively), helped to shape the format of this book. Finally, a special thank you to our families for their support.

Introduction

Whether you are an individual who suffers from a fear of heights, someone who has a loved one with a height phobia, or a therapist who works with people who fear heights, this book was written for you. The strategies described in this book have been around for decades and are well established as the most effective approaches for dealing with height phobia, as well as many other phobias. Although there are lots of books available on overcoming anxiety and phobias, this is the first book that specifically focuses on fear of heights.

In writing this book, we have described, in a self-help format, a treatment that has been used in numerous studies where people have successfully overcome their fear of heights with the help of a trained therapist. You may find that you are able to work through the techniques described in this book on your own. However, it is also possible that you will need some help or support from a friend, family member, or even a trained professional. Regardless of how you choose to use this book, if you are able to practice the exercises as described, you will likely experience relief from your fear of heights.

The Organization of This Book

This book has eight chapters. The first two chapters provide an overview of the nature and treatment of height phobia. Chapter 1 provides information about how prevalent height phobia is in the general population, as well as in particular groups (for example, among men versus women) and across different age groups. This chapter also discusses how this fear can affect your life and how you can successfully treat it with exposure therapy. Chapter 2 explores the causes of height phobia—including factors that can trigger a fear of heights initially, as well as factors that are thought to maintain the fear over time.

Chapters 3 and 4 provide information to help you prepare for treatment. In chapter 3, you will develop an exposure hierarchy, which is simply a list of situations that you fear, rank ordered with the easier situations at the bottom of the hierarchy and more challenging situations at the top. You will use the hierarchy as you work through the exposure exercises in chapter 5. Chapter 4 will help you locate the situations where you will do these exercises, and it will encourage you to identify a friend, family member, or other person who can help you as you confront your fear. It will also provide suggestions for deciding whether you should try to overcome your fear on your own or with the help of a professional.

The exposure techniques described in chapter 5 are the key to overcoming your fear. Exposure therapy works. In fact, it is the only treatment that has been shown to reliably work for height phobia. Although the other strategies described in this book may provide some relief, chances are that your largest gains will come from practicing the exposure-based exercises described here. Fortunately, these exposure practices can be complted at a pace that you will find manageable, and at no time will we recommend that you do anything that you aren't ready to try.

Chapter 6 provides tools that you can use to identify and challenge the anxiety-provoking thoughts that contribute to your fear. In chapter 7, you will learn about the factors that sometimes lead to a return of fear after someone has overcome a phobia, and you will learn about the best approaches for making sure that your fear doesn't come back. Finally, chapter 8 presents strategies that can be used to help someone else who has a fear of heights. If you suffer from a fear of heights, this chapter is for your helper—a friend or family member who can coach you during your exposure practices. If you are reading this book to help someone else who has a fear of heights, you should pay extra attention to chapter 8, though the entire book will be important for you to read.

How to Use This Book

We recommend that you begin by reading through the entire book once, without stopping to complete any of the exercises. This can probably be done within a few hours. This initial reading will give you an overview of the treatment and will help you to begin thinking about how you can use the proposed strategies to deal with your own fear. Next, we recommend reading the book again, this time completing all of the exercises. Some chapters can be read fairly quickly. You will probably get through the first two chapters in under an hour. Other chapters will take more time. Chapter 3 may take you a couple of hours to work through, if you include the time that it takes to develop your exposure hierarchy. You should spend the most time on chapter 5. The exposure practices described in chapter 5 may take you a few weeks to complete, assuming you practice almost daily.

Obtaining a Journal

The strategies described in this book require you to monitor your progress as you work on overcoming your fear. Many chapters include exercises that will require you to answer questions and record various types of information. Therefore, you will need to pick up some sort of journal or notebook to complete the exercises. Before beginning the first chapter, be sure to have your journal ready. Or, if you prefer, you can monitor your progress electronically, using a desktop, notebook, or handheld computer.

One More Thing...

Of course, just reading this book will not lead to a significant change in your fear of heights, any more than reading a book on weight loss will cause you to shed pounds. The key to reducing your fear will be to carry out the exercises described here and to actually change the way you behave in response to your fear. Specific phobias (including height phobia) are quite treatable. With some effort, there is no reason why your own fear cannot become significantly reduced in a relatively brief period. Good luck!

1

About Height Phobia

Ross was terrified of heights for as long as he could remember. Ever since childhood, he'd avoided roller coasters and Ferris wheels, skiing, standing on high balconies, and hiking in high places. He felt unsteady in these situations and feared that he might slip and fall. Although his fear affected the types of activities he could enjoy, it was never really a big problem until he got married and had children of his own. Ross's wife loved hiking, and he had promised her that they would go hiking together after they were married. His fear prevented him from following through on his promise. Also, his children loved amusement park rides and Ross was unable to ride with them, another source of embarrassment and distress for Ross. What finally led Ross to seek treatment was when his wife's parents moved into the penthouse of a high-rise condominium and Ross wasn't able to visit them.

Harpreet developed her fear of heights at the age of thirty-five. Her fear began suddenly when she was driving over the Claiborne Pell Newport Bridge during a vacation in Newport, Rhode Island. She was in the right-hand lane of the bridge and traffic was moving slowly. She began to feel panicky. Her heart was pounding and she felt very dizzy. She was sure she was going to lose control of the car and drive right off the bridge and into the water. It took all of her concentration to stay focused on getting to the other side. Returning from her vacation, she avoided the bridge entirely, taking another route. When she got home, she found herself avoiding local bridges that previously were never a problem for her. In fact, all elevated highways and roads had now become impossible for her to drive on. Many of the roads in her area had sections with steep drop-offs, so her new fear was making it difficult to go anywhere. She was fine in high places, as long as she wasn't driving (she had no trouble standing on a balcony), and she was fine driving, as long as the road wasn't elevated. It was specifically situations that involved a combination of height and driving that she found difficult. When Harpreet began treatment, she was spending an extra thirty minutes per day in the car, going out of her way to drive on roads that didn't include any elevated sections.

Vanessa avoided high places of all types, for fear that she would be drawn to the edge and jump off. She avoided balconies, fire escapes, bridges, rooftops, and the second floor of her local shopping mall. She avoided high places that were glassed in, even though she knew that she couldn't fall through the glass. Although she felt comfortable in regular elevators, glass elevators and escalators were a problem. She also avoided large staircases if they didn't have walls on both sides to block her view. Although she clearly didn't want to jump from high places (she was not feeling suicidal), when she was in a high place, she felt strangely pulled to the edge, and she didn't trust herself not to jump. It was easier to avoid heights altogether. Vanessa's fear prevented her from visiting certain friends, and it also affected her job. She worked as a real estate agent and had to avoid showing certain homes (ones with open staircases, for example).

These three people all experience fear of high places, one of the most basic of all fears. From as early as six to ten months of age, human infants are able to perceive sudden drops in the surface of the ground and will avoid such drops. Experiments with a variety of animals, including chicks, lambs, goats, pigs, cats, and dogs, show that the ability to perceive a change in distance to the ground (in other words, a drop) tends to appear when an animal is able to stand on its own, and all of the animals studied develop a tendency to be cautious around heights, though the age at which the caution develops varies from species to species (Gibson and Walk 1960). In the case of chicks, avoidance of sudden drops tends to begin at an age of less than twenty-four hours. Clearly, we don't have to learn to fear heights—caution in high places seems to be something that we develop automatically. That is not to say that excessive or extreme fears cannot be learned. We will return to the issue of how fears of heights develop in chapter 2.

So, if it is normal to have a respect for heights, why might it be important to consider overcoming such a fear? The goal of this book is not for you to end up with no fear of high places. Some degree of apprehension is useful for preventing you from taking risks that are potentially dangerous. A fear of heights is only a problem if it bothers you, or if it interferes with your ability to do the things that you want to do. For Ross, Harpreet, and Vanessa, fear of heights was clearly a problem.

What Is a Height Phobia?

The term *phobia* has a very specific definition, according to the fourth edition of the *Diagnostic and Statistical Manual of Mental Disorders* (American Psychiatric Association 2000). To be considered a phobia, a fear of heights must have a number of features, of which two are particularly important. First, the fear must be excessive or unrealistic. In other words, your level of fear must be out of proportion to a situation's actual danger. Second, the fear must cause significant distress or impairment. In other words, you must find the fear to be bothersome, or the fear must interfere with aspects of your functioning at work, in relationships, or in other important domains of living. So, a fear that rarely comes up, doesn't bother you, and doesn't cause significant problems in your life would not be considered a phobia.

Height phobia is considered to be a type of specific phobia. The term *specific phobia* refers to a phobia of a specific object or situation. In addition to height phobia, phobias of snakes, spiders, dogs, blood, needles, storms, flying, and other specific situations are often diagnosed as specific phobias. The technical name for a phobia of heights is *acrophobia*, though most experts tend to use the terms *height phobia* or *specific phobia of heights* to describe the problem. Height phobia can overlap with other phobia types, sometimes making it difficult to know what to call a particular individual's fear. For example, Harpreet's fear had features of both a *driving phobia* and a height phobia (neither term alone would adequately describe her problem).

Features of Height Phobia

Like all phobias, height phobia is associated with three main types of responses: feelings of anxiety, fear, and panic; phobic thinking; and phobic behavior. Each of these is described in the following sections.

ANXIETY, FEAR, AND PANIC

Depending on the situation, a person's reaction to a phobic stimulus can range from mild levels of anxiety and fear to a full panic attack. Although the terms anxiety, fear, and panic are often used interchangeably, there are subtle differences that are worth noting. *Anxiety* is an emotion focused on the possibility of threat at some point in the future. It is associated with a tendency to worry and to anticipate possible danger from the situation. If you are afraid of heights, anxiety is the feeling you might have when you think about having to attend a function at a rooftop restaurant later in the day. Anxiety is associated with various physical feelings, such as muscle tension, headaches, dizziness, and a racing heart.

In contrast, *fear* is a basic emotion that occurs when you interpret a situation as being an immediate threat. Fear is the feeling that you might experience if a bear were chasing you, or if you were about to hit another car while driving. If you have a height phobia, you probably experience the emotion of fear whenever you are in a high place that you find challenging.

The emotion of fear is sometimes described as one side of the *fight-or-flight response*. Whenever an organism is confronted with an immediate threat (or more accurately, a perceived immediate threat), the body reacts with a characteristic response that enables the organism to escape from the situation (flight) or to react aggressively to the source of the threat (fight). When people have height phobia, the more typical response is one of escape and avoidance. The fight-or-flight response includes a number of physical sensations that function to protect the body from the perceived threat. When you are frightened, your heart pumps more strongly and quickly to facilitate escape. Your rate of breathing increases in order to get more oxygen into your body. You sweat to cool off, so you can perform more efficiently. Other sensations that often occur as part of a fear response include dizziness, unsteadiness, or light-headedness; trembling or shaking; choking feelings; chest discomfort; numbness or tingling sensations; nausea; feeling unreal or detached; chills; and hot flushes.

The term *panic attack* is a clinical term that refers to a rush of fear that increases quickly (peaking in ten minutes or less) and that includes at least four out of a list of thirteen symptoms. Panic attack symptoms may include the physical sensations described earlier (racing heart, dizziness, breathlessness, and so on), as well as fears of dying, losing control, or going crazy. Of course, people do not actually die, lose control, or go crazy during panic attacks. They just feel as though they might. Typically, panic attack symptoms subside in anywhere from a few minutes to an hour or so, though they often subside very quickly if you leave the situation. Although panic attacks are usually triggered by a feared situation, they can also occur out of the blue. That was true for Harpreet. She experienced an unexpected panic attack in a situation that previously was not a problem for her, and the experience triggered her fear of heights. Panic attacks without an obvious trigger are common in another anxiety disorder called *panic disorder*.

PHOBIC THINKING

Height phobia tends to be associated with *phobic thinking*, or negative thoughts about the dangers of being in high places. If you truly believe that you are unlikely to fall from a high place and that the situation is safe, you won't be afraid. On the other hand, if you believe that the balcony is unsteady and that you are likely to fall, it's no wonder that you experience anxiety and fear. Some examples of common thoughts that can contribute to a fear of heights include the following:

- *If I am in a high place, I will be drawn to the ledge and jump.*

- *I will lose my balance and fall.*

- *If I stand too close to the railing on a balcony, someone will accidentally push me over.*

- *The structure of the bridge is unstable.*

- *If I fall from that height, I will be seriously hurt.*

- *The elevator will fall.*

- *My fear will cause me to get dizzy and fall.*

- *I will get so scared that I will faint or have a heart attack.*

- *I will lose control or go crazy from my fear.*

Note that several of the thoughts in this list are actually thoughts relating to the experience of fear itself, not the situation. Height phobia is associated with a fear of high places, but it is also associated with a fear of the physical sensations that occur when in a high place.

The thoughts that accompany your fear may be so quick and automatic that you are not aware of them. But with practice, it should get easier to identify the specific thoughts that are associated with your own height phobia. Chapter 6 discusses strategies for identifying and changing the thoughts that contribute to your fear. If you are unable to identify any specific anxiety-provoking thoughts, don't be alarmed, however. The most important strategies in this book (in chapters 3, 4, and 5) do not require you to know why you are afraid. Regardless of the thoughts beneath your fear, repeated exposure to feared situations will lead to a decrease in your fear.

PHOBIC BEHAVIOR

The emotion of fear is almost always accompanied by a strong desire to engage in some sort of behavior to reduce the fear. In most cases, the behavioral response is one of avoidance or escape. People who fear high places typically try to avoid being up in tall buildings, on balconies, near railings, in high seats in theaters and sports stadiums, and on elevated roads. Some people who fear heights may also avoid watching other people in high places or avoid even looking up at tall buildings while standing on the ground.

When forced to be in a high place, people with height phobia typically engage in safety behaviors designed to reduce their perception of risk or the feelings of fear. When on a balcony or some other elevated place, for example, they often avoid getting close to the edge, looking over the edge, or allowing anyone else to get close, for fear of being knocked off their feet. They may also hold on tightly to a railing or other fixed object. When driving on elevated roads with multiple lanes, they may purposely drive in the left lane. When flying, they may choose an aisle seat to avoid having to see out the window.

Although these behaviors are meant to ward off possible harm, their effect over the long term is to help maintain the phobia. As you will hear repeatedly throughout this book, overcoming your fear of heights will require you to confront the situations you fear and to let go of many of the safety behaviors that you use to protect yourself in these situations.

FEELING DRAWN TO THE EDGE

Another feature of height phobia that sometimes occurs is a feeling of being drawn to the edge. Some people who fear heights feel as though they might lose control and jump from a high place. This feeling is completely normal and is not an indication that you are really at risk of jumping. Of course, in rare cases, people sometimes do purposely jump off high places, but not because they have a height phobia. People who are feeling extremely depressed and suicidal may jump from bridges, windows, or balconies as a way of ending their lives. These events are typically planned in advance and are a tragic response to the hopelessness that accompanies severe depression. You may also have seen stories in the media of individuals who have jumped off rooftops believing that they could fly—these events are likely related to a serious mental illness, like schizophrenia or bipolar disorder, or perhaps to the use of hallucinogenic drugs. We are aware of no cases in which the urge to jump has actually led someone with a height phobia to jump from a high place.

Who Develops Height Phobia?

In a survey of more than eight thousand Americans (Curtis et al. 1998), fear of heights was found to be the second most prevalent type of specific fear, with only fears of animals being more common. Fear of heights was more prevalent than fears of flying, enclosed spaces, being alone, storms, blood, or water, for example. In this survey, about one in five people reported having an excessive fear of heights at some point in their lives, though many of these were not severe enough to warrant a diagnosis of specific phobia. In the same study, 5.3 percent of the individuals were found to suffer from a full-blown phobia of heights. These findings are similar to those from a large European study (Fredrikson et al. 1996), which found height phobia to be the most frequently diagnosed specific phobia, with 7.5 percent of the sample reporting a phobia of heights. The bottom line is that height phobia is very common, and milder fears of heights are even more prevalent. If you fear heights, you are not alone.

For many phobias, prevalence rates tend to be significantly higher for women than for men. For example, 80 percent or more of individuals with animal and insect phobias are women (Fredrikson et al. 1996). However, in the case of height phobia, differences between the sexes are not so pronounced. In the study by Fredrikson and colleagues, the rate of height phobia was slightly higher in women (8.6 percent) than in men (6.3 percent), but this difference was not statistically meaningful. Furthermore, there is evidence that men are more likely than women to underreport their fears (Pierce and Kirkpatrick 1992), so it is possible that the rates of height phobia are even more similar in men and women than those reported by Fredrikson and colleagues.

On average, height phobia tends to have a later onset than do some other phobias, like fears of animals, needles, and storms, but an earlier onset than others, such as driving phobia. Antony, Brown, and Barlow (1997) found that people with height phobia recalled first experiencing the fear at an average age of around twenty. In addition, they found that it often takes a few years for the fear to reach a level where it causes enough impairment to warrant a diagnosis of phobia. Despite the average onset age of twenty, it is important to note that height fears often begin in childhood or adolescence, and for some people, the fear can begin later in life.

Although the prevalence of many phobias (enclosed places, flying, dentists, and others) seems to be the same across different age groups, Fredrikson et al. (1996) found that height phobia tends to be more prevalent and more intense in older adults than in younger adults. Kirkpatrick (1984) found that the relationship between fear of heights and age was complex and that it differed between men and women. Among women, the fear of looking down from high buildings was higher in older adults than in younger adults, but the frequency of height phobia on the ground seemed to increase with age, until about age forty-five, and then it became less prevalent as people grew older. For men, there was no consistent pattern between severity of height phobia and age. Although this study is interesting, it is important not to read too much into its results, as they remain to be replicated by other researchers. A single study may find a particular result for many different reasons, including the ways in which questions were asked.

The Impact of Height Phobia

In some cases, a fear of heights can have a relatively small impact on a person's life. For example, if you only fear heights in the context of hiking through mountains, and you have no interest or need to be hiking through the mountains, then you don't have a problem. At the other extreme, a height phobia can affect someone's life almost every day. For example, if you live and work in a large city, it may be difficult to avoid meetings and appointments on high floors. You may be unable to easily avoid bridges, glass elevators, escalators, staircases, and railings. If you fear a wide range of situations involving heights, you may find that your phobia affects your ability to get around, the types of jobs you can accept, the sorts of recreational activities you can pursue, and even the places where you can shop.

Overcoming a fear of heights requires a strong commitment and a willingness to confront the situations you fear. Your decision to overcome your fear should depend in part on how much the fear affects your life from day to day. The greater the impact on your ability to do the things that you want to do, the more important it will be to work on overcoming your fear.

Overcoming Height Phobia

Fortunately, specific phobias are among the most treatable of problems that a person can have. Research on treating height phobia has focused primarily on exposure therapy, which involves gradually confronting feared situations. When done properly, exposure to high places almost always leads to a reduction in fear and avoidance. Exposure therapy begins with identifying the situations that you fear and avoid, as well as the factors that affect your level of fear in these situations. This information is used to help you generate a hierarchy of feared situations, as described in chapter 3. This hierarchy is a list of feared situations ranked in order of difficulty, with easier items on the bottom and the most difficult items at the top. Your treatment begins with exposure to easier items, followed by exposure to more difficult items. Chapter 5 describes the process of exposure therapy in detail and also reviews some of the research on exposure therapy for height phobia.

This book also addresses how to change your anxiety-provoking thoughts (see chapter 6). The techniques proposed here are useful for a variety of different types of anxiety-based problems and may help you with your fear of heights as well. These techniques for changing thoughts are called *cognitive strategies* (the word "cognition" means thought). Cognitive therapy involves identifying your anxiety-provoking thoughts (for example, "the bridge will collapse") and considering all of the evidence for and against your beliefs. Using a number of different exercises, cognitive therapy can help you to come to more realistic conclusions about the situations you fear, replacing your anxiety-provoking thoughts with beliefs and predictions that are more likely to represent the true state of affairs.

Summary

This chapter provides an overview of the nature and treatment of height phobia. A height phobia is a fear of heights that is out of proportion to the true danger, and that causes significant distress and interference in a person's life. Like all phobias, the fear that people with height phobia experience is associated with a variety of physical sensations, such as dizziness, breathlessness, and a racing heart. Height phobia also tends to be associated with negative thoughts about the dangers of being in high places. Avoidance of heights and reliance on safety behaviors help to maintain the fear over time. Height phobia is among the most common of fears, occurring frequently in both men and women. Fortunately, this type of phobia is also very treatable. Exposure-based strategies are generally considered to be the treatment of choice.

2

Where Does Height Phobia Come From?

Anna was an active and enthusiastic stay-at-home mother of three. She had taken a break from a successful career as a lawyer to raise her children. She prided herself on her parenting abilities and enjoyed enrolling her young children in various activities and taking them on interesting outings. However, on one such outing at the aquarium, she experienced a panic attack while holding her six-month-old baby on a high lookout. Although nothing terrible happened, Anna was scared that she might faint and drop her baby. After this terrifying experience, she began to notice that she felt fearful and nervous whenever she had to take her children to high places.

Jeff was a university student who was terrified of being high up, including standing on chairs and stepladders in his apartment. He always had to ask his roommate to do any chore that involved getting on a chair, such as changing a lightbulb. Jeff was frustrated by his fear, but he couldn't figure out where it came from. He knew that his dad was a worrier and that his mom was afraid of things like storms and dentists, but he'd never had a bad or scary experience with ladders or high places.

Jane was a successful university professor who grew up with a grandmother who was afraid of heights. Jane remembered her grandmother always warning her to be careful when she climbed the jungle gym at the park. Whenever Jane as a child visited her grandmother's house, the door to the deck was locked, and Jane's grandmother would repeatedly remind her grandfather to make sure the kids didn't get out there, because they might fall and break their necks. As Jane finished school and started her career, she noticed that her fear of high places slowly began to get worse and worse.

As you can see from these examples, people with fears of heights develop their fears through different routes. Sometimes, the cause may be obvious. In other cases, people may have no idea how their fear began. This chapter explores some of the possible factors that may contribute to the development of height phobia.

The Role of Biology

Phobias and other anxiety-based problems often run in families. However, simply knowing that several family members share a particular fear doesn't tell us if the fear is genetically inherited; it might also be shared because phobias are acquired through experience, perhaps from watching other family members be fearful or through other forms of learning. Scientists often study twins to estimate the extent to which the transmission of phobias across family members is related to genetics versus environmental factors, such as learning. Specifically, they examine the likelihood of a twin having the same phobia as his or her sibling. Key to this research is the fact that identical twins are 100 percent genetically identical, whereas fraternal twins share only about 50 percent of their genetic makeup (just like any two siblings). Therefore, if a phobia is 100 percent genetically determined, we might expect identical twins to always share the same phobias and fraternal twins to share their sibling's phobias about 50 percent of the time. By studying the extent to which identical and fraternal twins share various types of phobias, scientists are able to estimate the extent to which genetics and environment each contribute to the transmission of phobias from one generation to the next.

A number of twin studies have examined the extent to which genetic factors predispose individuals to develop specific phobias. Generally, these studies suggest that there is a genetic contribution to the development of specific phobias, though this component may show up in a number of different ways (Kendler et al. 2001). In other words, what is inherited is an increased likelihood of becoming anxious or fearful in certain situations, but not necessarily the same situations as your parents. In the case of height phobia, in particular, the role of genetics is even less clear. Skre et al. (2000) found no genetic component in the development of natural environment fears, including fear of heights. Therefore, the most we can conclude is that genetic factors may increase the likelihood of a person fearing something, but there are other environmental or learned factors that play an important role in determining what the fear looks like and whether a particular phobia actually develops.

The Role of Learning and Experience

More than a half century ago, psychologist Orval Hobart Mowrer (1939, 1960) suggested that the process of developing and maintaining phobias involves two stages of learning. The first stage was believed to be responsible for the initial development of fear. According to Mowrer, fears begin when a person associates a particular object or situation with some sort of unpleasant experience. For example, being bitten by a dog may lead to a fear of dogs. Getting into a car accident may lead to a fear of driving. In the case of height phobia, experiences such as falling, almost falling, or experiencing uncomfortable physical sensations, such as vertigo, while in a high place may contribute to developing a fear of heights. Scientists refer to this process as *classical conditioning*.

The second stage in Mowrer's theory explains why fears continue over time, even in the absence of repeated negative experiences. In other words, it explains why a dog phobia that began with being bitten might persist even when you don't continue to get bitten by dogs. According to Mowrer, it is the avoidance of the feared situation that is responsible for keeping the phobia alive. When you avoid something scary, the relief you feel reinforces or strengthens the desire to avoid it. After all, why would you want to put yourself in a scary situation if you didn't have to? The downside of avoidance is that it keeps you from relearning that the situation is actually generally safe, thereby causing your fear to continue.

To summarize, Mowrer proposed that fears develop through some sort of negative experience in the feared situation and that they continue over time because people avoid the situation. There is support for elements of Mowrer's theory. In fact, fears sometimes begin as a result of a negative experience in the feared situation, and it is well established that avoidance interferes with your likelihood of overcoming your fear. However, Mowrer's theory cannot explain some important observations about phobias, including the fact that individuals with height phobia often cannot identify a specific experience where a height was paired with a scary or anxiety-provoking experience. Most of the time, a height phobia doesn't begin with some sort of trauma, such as falling from a high place. Also, it's quite common for people to have negative experiences in particular situations without developing a phobia. For example, most people who fall from a ladder don't develop a fear of heights.

In response to these observations, a psychologist named Stanley Rachman (1977) put forth a broader model of fear development. He suggested that fears can develop in several different ways, including direct experience, learning through observing others, and learning through acquiring information about the dangers of a situation. These pathways will be described in the following sections.

LEARNING THROUGH DIRECT EXPERIENCE

One way a fear of heights may begin is through actually having a frightening experience in a high place. For example, if someone fell from a high ladder or a ledge, that person might develop a fear of high places. Or if a person had a bad panic attack while on a balcony, he or she might begin to associate panicky feelings with high places and develop a phobia.

LEARNING BY OBSERVING OTHERS

People may learn to be fearful of heights by watching someone else be fearful or by seeing someone else have a negative experience with heights. For example, if you happened to see someone fall from a high place, you might acquire a fear of heights. Or if you always watched your parent be fearful in high places, you might develop a height phobia. One client of ours could remember her mother being in a state of near panic every time her father had to climb a ladder, even a stepladder inside the house. This client went on to develop her own fear of heights, perhaps as a result of observing her mother's fear.

LEARNING THROUGH INFORMATION

The third pathway to developing fear discussed by Rachman involves being exposed to information about a particular object or situation being dangerous. We are continuously plagued with information from people we know, along with movies, news stories, and media coverage, about frightening events. It is difficult to get through a week without being told of the dangers of one situation or another. Think about warnings that are printed on various products, safety briefings that occur at the start of every air flight, articles you read in magazines, and the words of caution that parents often give their children. Indeed, our society is notorious for emphasizing how scary and seemingly dangerous the world can be.

So it's easy to imagine that some people might acquire a fear of heights because they've been repeatedly told that heights are dangerous and scary. You could watch a series of news reports about how many people fall from balconies, ledges, or ladders and become terrified of heights as a result. Perhaps fearful parents actually teach their children to be afraid of heights ("stand back from the edge of that balcony, so you don't fall" or "you're not allowed to climb the monkey bars because you could fall and crack your head open"). Well-meaning adults may provide information about safety in a way that increases a child's chance of becoming fearful.

Of course, we are not saying that parents should stop warning their children of the dangers of heights. Nor are we blaming parents or the media for causing people's fears. Instead, we are suggesting that people may be affected by these warnings and messages in different ways. Information about safety may prevent some children from taking unnecessary risks and have no role in causing an excessive fear. The same information might lead to an excessive fear reaction in other children, perhaps based on their genetic makeup or their previous experiences. It is very difficult to predict who is likely to respond in what way to negative messages encountered on a day-to-day basis.

There is support for Rachman's model of fear development. Many phobic individuals can recall incidents involving direct experience, observational learning, and information about a feared object (e.g., Menzies and Clarke 1993; Merckelbach et al. 1992). However, not everyone with a height phobia can remember an experience that fits one of Rachman's three pathways. Thus, his model still cannot explain the development of all phobias. Nor can Rachman's model explain why many people do not develop fear though they have negative experiences with heights or are exposed to negative information.

Can a Fear of Heights Be Instinctive Instead of Learned?

If Rachman's three pathways aren't the whole story, what else could explain the development of a fear of heights? An Australian psychologist named Ross Menzies and his colleagues (e.g., Menzies and Clarke 1995; Poulton and Menzies 2002) proposed adding a fourth pathway to Rachman's model of fear development. They suggested that some fears may be innately present from a young age without any learning experiences at all. That is, heights (as well as certain other situations) may have become, through evolution, innately fear-provoking, for they often were dangerous, especially the cliffs, ledges, and other high places that our ancestors may have been exposed to prehistorically. Of course, today, the high situations most of us are exposed to are actually safe (balconies have railings; lookout points have barriers around them). But, if heights were once truly dangerous, it would have been advantageous for people to be fearful of them, which explains why some people might be born with a fear of heights. This theory suggests that for most people, these fears go away through normal developmental processes, which is why not everyone has a fear of heights. For others, these fears either never go away, or they surface following a stressful period.

Related to the idea that a fear of heights might be instinctive is the idea that some fears are easier to develop than others because they had implications for survival in our ancestors. This notion is commonly referred to as *preparedness*. Martin Seligman (1971), the psychologist most associated with this notion of preparedness, proposed that we are all "prepared," or predisposed, to learn associations between certain stimuli and a fear response, but not others. Stimuli that are more likely to become phobic objects are those that have implications for survival (such as heights, snakes, and spiders). Cook and Mineka (1989) found that although it was relatively easy to trigger a fear of snakes in monkeys that observed other monkeys responding fearfully to snakes, it was very difficult to induce a fear of flowers using the same procedure. Presumably, fear of flowers is harder to induce because monkeys are not instinctually prepared to be fearful of this stimulus. The idea that fear of heights is instinctual makes logical sense, but the preparedness theory cannot as easily explain the development of driving phobia or fear of doctors, since neither cars nor doctors existed in prehistoric times. Therefore, the idea that fear of heights is innate is useful to consider, but it is probably not the entire story.

Personality Factors and the Development of Phobias

Researchers have studied the possible influence of personality factors on the development of fear. The term *personality* refers to long-standing tendencies that influence a person's behavior across a wide range of situations. One personality trait that has been studied is a trait that is often referred to as *behavioral inhibition*. Behavioral inhibition is just a fancy term that refers to the tendency of individuals to withdraw from or overreact to new situations. Biederman et al. (1990) found that children who scored high on a measure of behavioral inhibition at twenty-one months of age were more likely than less inhibited toddlers to develop various phobias at seven or eight years of age. Behavioral inhibition may be one variable that increases a child's risk for developing phobias or other anxiety problems, in general. However, it is unknown whether behavioral inhibition increases the risk of height phobia, in particular.

Another personality variable that may be relevant is called *anxiety sensitivity*. This is a tendency to be frightened of the physical sensations associated with anxiety and fear (dizziness, breathlessness, racing heart) and to believe that these sensations are dangerous. If you believe that dizziness is going to lead to fainting or falling, you may be more likely to be fearful if you experience dizziness on a balcony or in another high place.

Research on anxiety sensitivity has found that people with specific phobias are generally no more anxious than people without phobias are about experiencing these physical sensations (Rapee et al. 1992). However, when people are asked how much they fear experiencing these sensations in the presence of their phobic object or situation, a different story emerges. They generally report elevated fear of these sensations. Furthermore, people with height phobia report a greater fear of their physical sensations during exposure to high places than people with animal phobias report during exposure to their feared animal (Antony, Brown, and Barlow 1997). In other words, people with animal phobias are primarily afraid of their feared animal and are not especially afraid of their racing heart and other physical sensations. However, people with height phobia are afraid not only of high places but also of the sensations they experience in the situation because of their fear.

Why Doesn't Height Phobia Go Away on Its Own?

You may have noticed that fears that reach the level of a phobia rarely spontaneously vanish. There are likely a number of explanations for this. One involves the use of avoidance as a coping strategy. As stated earlier, it makes a lot of sense that people who are afraid of heights would try to avoid high places that they find scary. Unfortunately, avoidance is only helpful in the short term, as it provides you with a sense of relief about not having to enter a feared situation ("Phew. I feel so much better now that I cancelled that appointment on the twenty-second floor"). In the long term, however, avoidance just makes your fear stick around. You never get a chance to learn that heights aren't as dangerous as they seem. You also don't get the opportunity to learn to cope with being in a high place.

Another explanation is that once a height phobia develops, people more often notice information that is consistent with their fear than information that is inconsistent with their fear. For example, you may have a clear memory of a frightening news story about someone falling from a ladder while you pay relatively little attention to the numerous people who successfully climb ladders every day without incident. This kind of bias toward negative or scary information about heights is thought to contribute to keeping your fear alive.

Exercise: Where Did Your Fear Come From?

Where do you think your fear came from? To figure this out, consider the following questions:

1. Have you had a scary experience with heights?

2. Have you seen someone have a scary experience with heights?

3. Does anyone in your family also have a fear of heights?

4. If so, is this someone with whom you've spent a lot of time and with whom you've had an opportunity to observe the fear (suggesting you could have learned your fear through observation)? Or is this someone you're related to but haven't spent a lot of time with (suggesting a possible genetic vulnerability)?

5. Do you remember learning that heights are a dangerous thing? For example, did you have a parent or teacher who told you that you should stay away from heights?

Don't worry if you can't identify the cause of your fear. The truth of the matter is that fear development is probably a complex interplay of genetics, experiences, and personality style. And the good news is that a fear of heights can be treated effectively even if you have no idea how it started. It's more important to understand the factors that keep your fear going, such as avoidance and focusing on scary information about heights.

Summary

This chapter provides some ideas of where height phobia may come from and how it develops. Most experts believe that fears and phobias develop through a complex interaction of biological and environmental factors. There is no single gene that parents pass to their children that causes a fear of heights. More likely, children inherit a tendency to be anxious, which can develop into any of a number of different types of fears, including fear of heights. People may develop a height phobia after having a frightening experience in a high place, after watching someone else have a frightening experience in a high place, or after being told that heights are dangerous or scary. Some researchers have argued that fear of heights is an easy phobia to develop because humans are prepared to develop this fear as a result of the true danger high situations posed in prehistoric times. Finally, a height phobia typically does not go away on its own. The tendency to avoid high places is one factor that contributes to the maintenance of your fear over time.

3

Developing a Hierarchy

So far, we have discussed the nature of height phobia and how this problem can develop. To get over your fear of heights, you will have to begin to confront your fears directly. We know this may sound scary, but don't put this book down just yet! Before actually confronting any frightening situations, there is an intermediate step to take that will help break down the process into manageable stages. This intermediate step is to develop an exposure hierarchy.

What Is a Hierarchy?

An exposure hierarchy is simply an ordered list of situations that you might typically avoid because of your fear. At the top of the hierarchy is the situation that scares you the most. At the bottom of the hierarchy is a situation that you find somewhat scary, but it's one that you could tackle right away, perhaps with some support. The in-between items, or steps, are situations of increasing difficulty. The hierarchy provides a road map for working on your fear. We all know that it is much easier to accomplish a large goal if we break it down into more manageable steps. This is the purpose of your exposure hierarchy.

We typically recommend that a hierarchy include between ten and fifteen items, though your hierarchy may have fewer than ten items if your fear of heights is limited to a few situations (for example, if you are chiefly afraid of riding a particular escalator at the mall). Your hierarchy can also have more than fifteen items, if the list of situations you fear is very long, but we recommend not having too many more than this number. Imagine trying to work on a goal when the goal involves twenty-five steps! You might be inclined to put off working toward your goal if it will take too long to get there. To make your hierarchy a reasonable length, we encourage you to limit it to situations that you would like to feel more comfortable in. If you are scared of being on top of a roof, but there's no need for you to do this in your life, don't include that situation. On the other hand, if your job requires you to be able to climb high ladders or work on rooftops, and you're afraid of getting on high ladders and rooftops, you will want to include these activities in your hierarchy.

You will give each situation on your hierarchy a number representing the fear level, or degree of fear, you would expect to experience if you were in that situation. It's helpful to use a scale of 0 to 100 points, with 0 being no fear and 100 being the most fear you can imagine. A rating of 50 would represent a moderate level of fear—definitely noticeable, but manageable. For each item, you can use any number ranging from 0 to 100. The number is a subjective rating, meaning that it represents your opinion of how scary a situation is. So there are no wrong numbers. A good rule of thumb is to make sure that the situations on your hierarchy are in the right order (from hardest at the top to easiest at the bottom) and that the numbers you give each situation seem like reasonable estimates of your fear.

A hierarchy should include situations with a broad range of fear ratings. In other words, a hierarchy shouldn't be limited to situations with ratings of 90, 95, or 100. That hierarchy would be too overwhelming for anyone to consider trying. We encourage you to include situations that are well spaced between easy (ratings between 20 and 30) to difficult (ratings between 90 and 100). Below are two examples of hierarchies. One is for Peter, a thirty-eight-year-old man with a wide-ranging fear of heights. The other is for Julia, a forty-three-year-old woman with a more specific fear of high bridges. As you may notice, Julia's hierarchy is shorter than Peter's, because her fear of heights is restricted to two local bridges. You may also notice that Julia's hierarchy includes going over the same two bridges, but doing it at different times of day and with and without her husband. There are probably a number of factors that make a situation more or less difficult for you, and these factors can be included in your hierarchy. Possible factors that may affect your fear of heights are discussed in more detail below.

Example: Peter's Exposure Hierarchy

Item	Description	Fear Rating (0–100)
1	*Standing on the outdoor observation deck of the CN Tower*	*100*
2	*Standing on the indoor lookout of the CN Tower*	*90*
3	*Sitting on the rooftop terrace of my office building*	*85*
4	*Standing by the picture windows on the twenty-fifth floor of my office building*	*70*
5	*Climbing a ladder to the second story of my house*	*65*
6	*Looking over the balcony of a sixth-floor apartment*	*60*
7	*Climbing a ladder to the top of my shed*	*50*
8	*Standing on a stepladder to change a lightbulb*	*40*
9	*Climbing the jungle gym with my son*	*35*
10	*Looking over my deck railing*	*30*

Example: Julia's Exposure Hierarchy

Item	Description	Fear Rating (0–100)
1	*Driving over the Burlington Skyway Bridge after dark, alone*	*100*
2	*Driving over the Burlington Skyway Bridge during the day, alone*	*90*
3	*Driving over the Burlington Skyway Bridge during the day, with husband*	*70*
4	*Driving over the Peace Bridge after dark, alone*	*60*
5	*Driving over the Peace Bridge during the day, alone*	*55*
6	*Driving over the Peace Bridge during the day, with husband*	*40*

Developing a List of Feared Situations

The first step in developing your own hierarchy is to brainstorm a list of the situations you fear. Try not to limit yourself. Record all the situations involving heights that you fear. Later, you can choose the most important situations from this list to put on your hierarchy. When making your list, be sure to include the most difficult situations you fear, even if you can't imagine being able to handle them right now. For example, when Peter was working on his hierarchy, he couldn't imagine ever being able to stand on the outdoor observation deck of the CN tower, which is a whopping 114 stories tall. At first, he didn't want to include standing on the observation deck, because he thought he would never be able to do this, but then he decided to do so as part of a wish list of situations he wanted to work on. Peter often had out-of-town guests or business associates who wanted to see this world-renowned landmark, and Peter always had to make an excuse about why he couldn't go or why he would have to wait at the bottom of the tower while his guests enjoyed themselves without him. By including the deck as a situation on his hierarchy, he left open the possibility of working on this situation in treatment.

Exercise: Develop a List of Feared Situations

In your journal, make a list of all the situations you avoid because of your fear of heights. Think about the situations that come up all the time, as well as those that don't come up very often but are important to you (for example, riding on a Ferris wheel at the annual fair). If you're having trouble thinking of situations, ask someone who knows you for suggestions. They may have noticed other situations that are bothersome to you. For now, don't worry about how many situations you've identified, or about putting these situations in any particular order, but simply write down all your ideas. To help you further prepare for treatment, chapter 4 includes examples of high places that people with height phobia often avoid. You will have an opportunity to add to your hierarchy after reading that chapter.

Identifying Factors That Influence Your Fear

There are many factors that can make a particular situation more or less frightening. As you may have noticed in Julia's hierarchy, the time of day and presence of a supportive person made a difference to her fear ratings. It is useful to consider the factors that might influence your fear. Some factors include the following:

- Presence of a supportive person or someone you know

- Presence of a stranger

- If it is light or dark (how much can you see over the edge if you are looking down)

- If the situation is contained (like a balcony with a railing or a room with a window) or open (like a ladder or the edge of a cliff or hill)

- Distance from the ground

- Distance from the edge of the drop-off

- Presence of movement (for example, a bird flying by)

- Presence of distracting noise

- Whether it is windy

- Type of floor (for example, a solid step versus a step that you can see through)

- Stability or shakiness of the ground

- Slope of the ground (flat versus sloping down toward the edge)

- Whether you are walking, in a car, or in another type of vehicle (airplane, train, or other)

- Whether you are holding on to something

- Whether you are standing or sitting

- Where you are looking

- Your physical feelings (for example, feeling light-headed or dizzy)

Exercise: List the Variables That Affect Your Fear

In your journal, make a list of all the factors that influence your fear by either increasing or decreasing your discomfort in the situations that you fear.

Generating Your Hierarchy

You are now ready to make your own hierarchy. Look at your original list of feared situations. Start by putting a star (*) next to the ones that are most problematic, that come up often, or that are important for you to work on. Pick up to ten or fifteen situations that you think should be on your hierarchy. Next, try to make the items on your list as descriptive and detailed as possible, taking into account the factors that influence your level of fear in each case. Try to incorporate these variables into your list by modifying items to include these factors. Here are a few examples of how to modify items to make them more detailed:

Original Item:	*Balconies*
Modified Item:	*Standing on the balcony of Jim's apartment building (sixth floor), by myself*
Original Item:	*Amusement park rides*
Modified Item:	*Riding the mini Ferris wheel at "Funland" during the day, with my husband*

Once you have a good list of possible situations for your hierarchy, give each one a number from 0 to 100, representing the fear you would expect to feel if you were to go into this situation. Remember, on this scale, 0 points would mean no fear and 100 points would mean the most fear you could imagine. When fear ratings are complete, put the items in order, with the most frightening item at the top. Next, review your list:

1. Are your hierarchy items sufficiently detailed? Have you considered all the factors that affect your fear levels?

2. Do you have an appropriate number of situations (ideally, ten to fifteen)? If you have fewer than ten items, is it possible for you

to divide some of the situations into multiple items by varying the factors that affect your fear? (For example, changing the item "stand on a ladder" into two items—"stand on the third step of a ladder" and "stand on the fifth step of a ladder.") If you have many more than fifteen situations, can you cut out a few situations that are less important for you to work on?

3. Do you have a good range of fear ratings, including items close to 100, items close to 30, and items representing a wide range in between?

4. Are the situations on your hierarchy practical? Will you be able to practice them if you want to? If an item involves, say, going to a specific bridge that is hundreds of miles away in a place you never visit, perhaps pick a bridge that is closer to you, so you can actually practice there.

5. Are your situations safe to practice? Are they situations that most people who don't have a significant fear of heights would feel comfortable in?

Summary

The best way to overcome any fear is usually to tackle it head-on—an idea that is probably stressful and difficult to imagine. After all, if it were easy to confront your fear, you would have done it already and wouldn't need to read this book! To make the process of confronting high places more manageable, it is useful to break down your fear into smaller steps. In this chapter, you learned how to construct an exposure hierarchy, a list of your feared situations ranked in order from most to least frightening. In the remaining chapters, you will use your hierarchy to guide your treatment, which will involve working on less scary situations before tackling the scarier ones.

4

Preparing for Treatment

So far, you've learned about the nature and causes of height phobia, and you've developed a list of high places that you fear and avoid. You're almost ready to start your treatment. But first there are a few other issues that need to be discussed. This chapter will help you explore your level of motivation and commitment to overcoming your fear. It will help you to set goals and find a helper who can coach you during the practices. It will also suggest ideas for situations where you can practice exposure, and it will help you develop an exposure schedule. Finally, this chapter discusses strategies to decide whether you might be better off working with a therapist and, if so, how to find an appropriate professional who is qualified to help you with this problem.

Making a Commitment to Change

Before you try to overcome your fear of heights, take a moment to examine whether you are ready, willing, and able to make this change:

1. Is making this change important to you?

2. Of the various things on your plate right now, is overcoming your fear of heights a high priority?

3. Are you willing to experience some discomfort in the short term to feel some relief later?

4. Are you confident in your ability to change?

You may be ambivalent or unsure about making changes—even positive ones. After all, change often comes at a cost. Possible costs of going through the treatment in this book may include the time it will take you to complete the exercises, the discomfort you may experience along the way, the possibility of not reaching your goals, and a risk of later experiencing increased pressure from others to do things that you really don't want to do (after all, until now you may have been able to rely on your fear as a reason for not doing certain things, like fixing the roof). If you choose to work with a professional therapist, there may be a financial cost as well.

Before we talk you into completely giving up, however, you also might want to consider some of the advantages of overcoming your fear. There may be certain practical benefits, such as possible financial gains if your job depends on your going into high places. You'll also feel less pressure from others to confront feared situations. But it is even more important to consider your internal reasons for making the change. Is overcoming your fear of heights something that will allow you to live more fully, according to values that are important to you? Are there activities that you really want to do but can't do because of your phobia of heights? Would making this change enhance your relationships or your enjoyment of work? Would overcoming your fear take away a big source of stress in your life? Would your sense of accomplishment be worth the temporary discomfort that you may experience along the way?

Not everyone who fears heights should necessarily work on getting over the fear. If the places you fear rarely arise, your fear doesn't cause you that much stress, or if you don't care that there are certain situations you can't enter, then it probably isn't important to overcome your fear. On the other hand, if your fear of heights bothers you, or if it stops you from doing things that you want to do, then overcoming your fear may be worth it. The strategies in this book can work well if you are committed to making a change. If you use the exercises in this book as described, you should notice a significant decrease in your fear.

Exercise: Consider the Advantages vs. the Disadvantages

In your journal, record your responses to the following questions:

1.   What are the advantages and disadvantages of having things stay the way they are now? What are some of the benefits of having your fear? What problems does the fear create in your life?

2.   What are the advantages and disadvantages of overcoming your fear of heights? What would your life be like if this fear were suddenly gone? Can you remember a time when you weren't afraid of heights? What was your life like then?

3.   Do you believe that you can make this change if you work hard at it? How confident are you that the strategies in this book will be effective for you? What personal strengths do you have that will make it possible to overcome your fear?

4.   Are you willing to make this change?

Setting Goals

Well, if you are still reading, we will assume that you're going ahead with the program described in this book. In other words, you have decided to overcome your fear of heights. So, how will you measure your success? The only way to assess whether your treatment has worked is to identify goals and to pay attention to whether you achieve them.

There are many different types of goals. Goals may be *emotional* in nature (for example, to experience no more than mild fear while driving on elevated roads), or they may be more *behavioral* (to be able to climb a ladder, regardless of your level of fear). Often, before reaching your emotional goals, you will first need to meet your behavioral goals. That is, being able to stand on a balcony without experiencing fear will first require you to stand on the balcony while experiencing fear.

Goals can be very *specific* (to stand on a fire escape with minimal fear), or more *general* (to be more satisfied in your relationships and work). In setting your goals, be sure to include at least some that are relatively specific. Specific goals have a number of advantages over general goals. They are often easier and quicker to reach, and it is usually easier to recognize when you have reached a specific goal (it is easier to measure whether you are fearful on a glass elevator than to know, more generally, if you have improved your enjoyment of life). Also, with more specific goals, it is often easier to develop a treatment plan. That is not to say that you should not include general goals. Just make sure that some of your treatment goals are specific.

You should also distinguish between goals that are *short term* versus goals that are *long term*. If you are afraid of almost all high places, it may not be realistic to assume that you will overcome all of your fears in a week or two. However, it may be realistic to assume that within a couple of weeks, you will overcome your fear of standing on a balcony. Conquering your fears in a wider range of situations may take a few weeks or perhaps months.

Exercise: Write Down Your Goals

In your journal, make a list of goals for your treatment. First, list your long-term goals (perhaps goals for a year from now). Next, list some shorter-term goals that will help you along the road to meeting your long-term goals. As you try to generate goals, consider what you would like to be different (with respect to your fear of heights) a week from now, a month from now, three months from now, six months from now, or a year from now. You can even set goals for five years from now.

Finding a Helper

Almost all of the research on overcoming specific phobias has been based on treatment with a trained therapist. If you end up using this book while you are in therapy with a professional, then your therapist will likely help you plan the treatment and coach you during your exposure practices. If you are planning to work on your own, you may still find it useful to have someone assisting you, particularly if you find it difficult to spend a lot of time in the situations you fear. We recommend that you identify someone who can work with you as a helper or coach. Your helper can be a spouse, friend, family member, or anyone who has the following qualities:

- Someone you trust and around whom you are willing to let your fear show

- Someone who is willing to spend time with you during exposure practices (particularly early in treatment)

- Someone who is willing to learn about the strategies for overcoming height phobia by reading this book (especially chapter 8)

- Someone who is likely to be patient, supportive, and encouraging, but not overly pushy or nagging

- Someone who will not become frustrated or angry if you have difficulty confronting a feared situation

- Someone who will not trivialize your anxiety or belittle you for having this problem

- Someone who is not afraid of high places and who can model or demonstrate non-fearful behavior during your exposure practices

- Someone who will follow your lead and who will never use force, deception, or surprise to get you to do things that you don't feel ready to try

Having a helper to work with you on your fear has the same function as exercising with a personal trainer or a friend. Your helper will help motivate you and will make sure that you push yourself as much as you are willing and able to push. Your helper will also give you positive feedback on your successes, reminding you of how far you have come. Finally, he or she can help you generate ideas for possible practices.

If you don't have a friend or family member who can play this role, don't worry. As long as you are willing to complete the exercises described in this book, your fear of heights should improve. Although exposure treatment is easier if you have a helper, having a helper is useful but not necessary (just as it is useful, though not necessary, to have a personal trainer work with you if you are trying to get more physically fit).

Locating Situations Where You Can Practice

This section reviews situations—organized by type of high place—where you can complete your exposure practices. If any of these situations is difficult for you, you may want to consider adding them to your exposure hierarchy.

OPEN INDOOR HEIGHTS

If you are afraid of open heights indoors, consider visiting a theater or sports stadium. You may be able to get permission to enter the arena or theater when it is not open to the public. Otherwise, you may need to attend an official event. If so, we recommend that you buy the worst tickets available (those highest up) and that you arrive as early as possible, so you can practice your exposure while the lights are still on (especially if being able to see how high up you are is important for triggering your fear). Another possibility is finding a tall building with an open atrium in the center. For example, some hotels are built like hollow shells, so you can be on a high floor and look all the way down to the bottom in the center of the building. You may also consider visiting a tall, narrow shopping mall with a large atrium, if there is one in your community. Some office buildings, museums, and other public buildings have an open concept or hollow design, so you can be up high on the inside of the building and look down.

OPEN OUTDOOR HEIGHTS

You may consider hiking near a cliff or ledge, or on a mountain or hill. Or, you can find a bridge to stand on or walk over. You can also stand on a balcony in a tall residential building, stand on a rooftop, or stand on a fire escape located on the outside of a building. A number of recreational activities offer opportunities for exposure, including skiing, riding a ski lift, diving off a diving board, and going on certain amusement park rides. Of course, make sure that you are allowed in these open spaces and that you are not doing something that anyone would consider dangerous, such as standing right on the edge of a cliff, without a railing, or illegally climbing onto the rooftop of a building.

OTHER SITUATIONS INVOLVING HEIGHTS

Some people with height phobia are fearful of watching others in high places or of looking up at tall buildings when standing on the ground. For others, watching films or videos depicting heights, like the movie *Cliff Hanger*, can trigger fear. Elevators are often difficult, particularly elevators with glass windows. Other challenging situations include riding escalators and climbing certain staircases, using indoor rock-climbing walls, standing on chairs, ladders, or stepstools, driving in high places, or looking down the center of a stairwell in a tall building. You may want to consider adding some of these situations to your hierarchy if they are difficult for you.

Exercise: List Places Where You Can Practice

In your journal, list places where you are afraid to go in your own city or neighborhood. Are there particular places where you can plan to practice exposure? Consider updating or revising your exposure hierarchy if you have now thought of some additional places to practice that you hadn't thought of before.

Developing a Practice Schedule

The key to success is regular exposure practice. You won't need to continue frequent exposures forever, but for a short time (anywhere from a few weeks to a few months), it will be important to find one or two hours several times per week to practice confronting high places. The easiest way to make sure you complete practices is to schedule them in advance, just like you would any other appointment. Also, building some practices into your regular routine will help decrease the amount of extra time needed for practicing. If you have to run some errands, take routes that involve bridges or elevated roads if you can. If you are worried about changing your mind and not following through with your practices, arrange to have someone join you. Making a commitment to another person to go somewhere will increase the likelihood of completing the exposure practice.

Exercise: Schedule Practice Sessions

In your date book or calendar, set aside three or four two-hour practice times per week over the next month. You can always change the schedule later, if necessary.

When to Seek Professional Help

If you find that overcoming your fear on your own or even with your helper's assistance does not lead to the changes that you were hoping for, don't despair. Treatment with a trained therapist is still an option. In fact, in our experience, professional treatment for this particular phobia almost always works, provided the appropriate exposure-based strategies are used, the therapist has been trained to work with phobias using this particular type of treatment, and the client follows through with his or her homework exercises. If you decide to seek professional help, we recommend that you ask potential therapists a number of questions to make sure of the following:

Professional background. Ensure that the therapist has professional credentials, including an advanced degree, in a mental health–related discipline and has a license or registration to practice in your area.

Experience. Ensure that the therapist has experience treating anxiety disorders. Specific experience in treating phobias is also important, though it's not essential that your therapist has treated height phobia, in particular, since the treatments for various phobias are often similar.

Training. Ideally, your therapist will have received specific training in the treatment of anxiety disorders, preferably under supervision in a center that specializes in treating anxiety and related problems.

Therapeutic approach. Ensure that the therapist has training and experience in using exposure-based treatments. This treatment is sometimes also referred to as in vivo exposure, behavior therapy, or cognitive behavioral therapy (or CBT). Regardless of which of these names your therapist uses to describe the process, make sure that the treatment will include directly confronting your feared situations, as described in chapter 5. It is also helpful to know whether the therapist would accompany you on some of the exposure practices, since therapist-assisted exposure can often be useful, particularly early in treatment.

There are a few other things to keep in mind in choosing a therapist. A relatively new therapist, like a recently graduated psychologist, may be just as good as a therapist who has been practicing for years, as long as he or she has strong training and experience in exposure-based treatments. Also, it is very important that you feel comfortable with your therapist. If you meet with a therapist a few times and you find that you have difficulty "connecting" with him or her, it may be best to interview other therapists until you find a good match.

WHERE TO FIND AN EXPERIENCED THERAPIST

Finding an experienced therapist is sometimes a challenge. One option is to get in touch with an association whose members specialize in treating anxiety disorders. A good place to start is the Anxiety Disorders Association of America (ADAA), which may be accessed online at www. adaa.org or by phone at (240) 485-1001. The ADAA can provide referrals to professionals in many places throughout North America who are experienced in treating phobias. Through its Web site, you may be able to find an expert in your own community. The ADAA may be able to help you find similar associations in various countries around the world, such as the Anxiety Disorders Association of Canada (www.anxietycanada.ca). Some states and provinces have their own anxiety disorders associations as well.

There are also professional associations whose members have more general expertise in behavioral and cognitive therapies. In North America, the Association for Behavioral and Cognitive Therapies (ABCT) has several thousand members, many of whom have experience in treating anxiety-based problems, such as height phobia. Its Web site (www.abct.org) has a link that can help you find a therapist. A similar association in the United Kingdom is the British Association for Behavioural and Cognitive Psychotherapies (www.babcp.com).

Finally, speaking with a healthcare provider, such as a family doctor, or perhaps a therapist whom you or someone you know is seeing for another problem, may be a good way to get a referral to a professional in your area who specializes in treating anxiety disorders and phobias.

Summary

Before beginning your treatment, it will be useful to assess your level of motivation and commitment to overcoming your fear of heights. Once you have made a decision to go forward, the next step is to set goals. Being aware of your goals will allow you to develop a treatment plan that will get you to where you want to be. Setting goals will also allow you to measure your success in treatment. Sometimes it is difficult to overcome a significant phobia without help and support from others. We recommend that you work with a close friend or family member who can coach you during practices and offer support as you work on confronting the situations you fear. For some people, working with a professional therapist is the best way to overcome a phobia of heights. If you decide to seek professional help, it is important to find a therapist who has the training, skills, and experience to provide the most effective help possible.

5

Confronting Your Fear

This is the most important chapter in this book. Without exposing yourself to the places that make you uncomfortable, it is unlikely that you will ever notice a significant reduction in your fear. Exposure to high places has been found to be an effective treatment for height phobia in numerous studies published over the past few decades (Baker, Cohen, and Saunders 1973; Emmelkamp and Felten 1985; Lang and Craske 2000; Williams, Turner, and Peer 1985). In fact, we are aware of no studies that support treatments for this problem that don't include exposure as a component.

At least one study (Pendleton and Higgins 1983) found that even just imagining being in a high place could eventually lead to fear reduction. However, we recommend that your exposure involve confronting feared situations in real life (also called *in vivo exposure*), as opposed to confronting heights in your imagination. Live exposure tends to be more effective than exposure in the imagination (Emmelkamp and Wessels 1975). Of course, imaginary exposure may be a reasonable first step in rare cases where live exposure is impossible or too difficult. Also, some studies have found that computer-simulated exposures to high places using virtual reality (VR) can also lead to a reduction in fear. We will discuss VR treatments later in this chapter.

The key to overcoming your phobia is to confront your feared situations directly, rather than avoid them completely or use various safety behaviors to protect yourself when in high places. This chapter describes what you need to know to get the most you can out of exposure. It begins with a reminder of why avoidance is not the best approach for dealing with your fear over the long term. For those who fear physical sensations, such as dizziness, which may occur in high places, this chapter includes a section on exposure to feared sensations. It also includes a case illustration to bring the treatment procedures to life. Finally, a section on troubleshooting will help you cope with the obstacles that most commonly arise during exposure therapy.

Why Avoiding Heights Is Not a Solution

We are all motivated to avoid or escape from situations that make us feel uncomfortable. This tendency to avoid is a natural part of the fight-or-flight response that characterizes fear. The purpose of avoidance is to protect us from perceived danger or threat. Avoiding or escaping from a feared situation has the added effect of engendering feelings of comfort, well-being, or relief. In fact, the relief we experience when we leave an uncomfortable situation is thought to reinforce or strengthen our tendency to avoid things in the future. This avoidance can interfere with your ability to overcome your fear. Long-term comfort in high places will require you to begin confronting those places you fear.

In addition to paying attention to obvious forms of avoidance (leaving a situation completely), it is important to note more subtle forms of avoidance (going into a situation but standing away from the edge, gripping a railing or another person, making sure you are protected from the wind, not looking down, and so on). These subtle forms of avoidance (also called *safety behaviors*) can undermine the effectiveness of exposure therapy. Avoiding the physical sensations you experience in high places may also be a safety behavior. For example, sitting down on a balcony to avoid feeling dizzy may feel good in the short term, but over the long term, we recommend that you practice standing on the balcony until you no longer feel dizzy, or until you no longer care about the dizziness when it does occur.

Of course, if you can avoid the situations and sensations you fear and suffer no negative consequences, then there's no need to overcome your fear. However, the more you avoid situations, the greater the chances that this avoidance is interfering with your job, school, relationships, family life, hobbies, interests, recreation, or other activities. Basically, avoidance is a problem when the costs of avoiding outweigh the benefits.

What Happens During Exposure Therapy?

Starting an exposure program is like starting a new exercise program. It may take a while before you begin to see improvement. At first, your exposure sessions may be scary and tiring. You may notice an increase in anxiety, grumpiness, and fatigue. However, if you stick to your exposure schedule, these feelings will diminish over time.

Exposure practices typically begin with situations from the bottom half of your exposure hierarchy. We recommend that you start with whatever item you feel you can do. If you are willing to begin with an item near the middle of your hierarchy, then that's great. If not, it is perfectly fine to start with an item closer to the bottom. The key is to pick a practice that will be challenging but that you are willing to try.

Chances are that carrying out the practice will trigger a strong fear reaction at first. Your efforts should be aimed at staying in the situation. Over time, your fear will probably decrease. Each person responds differently, however. Your fear may decrease over a few minutes, or it may take an hour or longer. In fact, for some people, fear doesn't decrease at all over a particular practice (see the troubleshooting section at the end of this chapter). If your fear does decrease to a manageable level, it's your cue to increase the intensity or difficulty of the exposure and to stay at that level until your fear decreases again, or until you learn that your feared predictions don't come true.

An exposure practice might begin with you standing about three feet from a balcony railing while experiencing a fear level of about 80 out of 100. After about twenty minutes, your fear might decrease to a level of 50, at which point you would move about a foot closer to the edge. At this distance, your fear might shoot up to 90, though it might then decrease to about an 80 when you look straight ahead instead of looking down. As your fear becomes more manageable, you might then force yourself to look down. It might be difficult at first, but eventually, your fear might decrease to a 40. You might then move right to the edge of the balcony and hold on to the railing. Again, you would stay long enough in that location to learn that it is perfectly safe. The entire practice might last an hour or two, and the end result would likely be a significant reduction in fear.

During subsequent practices, you might try some of the same situations again (be aware that some fear may return between practices), in addition to trying some more difficult situations from your hierarchy. As you practice particular items, other items on your list should become easier to do, as well. You will make gradual progress, so by the time you get to the most difficult items on your list, they will seem like just another small step in your program. By that point, the top items won't seem nearly as difficult as they might have seemed before you started the treatment. The process is similar to the process of becoming physically fit. If you work up to it gradually, running a mile isn't nearly as difficult as it would be if you tried doing it after having done no exercise for years.

To summarize, exposure therapy requires you to make a commitment to experience fear and discomfort in the short term, so you can feel more comfortable in high places later. There will be bumps along the way. During some practices, your fear may not decrease. In fact, during some practices, your fear may be even higher than it was during earlier ones, especially if you are experiencing a lot of stress that particular day, perhaps from work. Nevertheless, your fear will most likely generally decrease over time. Exposure-based treatments for phobias are among the most effective treatments that are available for any psychological problems. Almost everyone who persists with exposure practices experiences a reduction in fear.

How to Get the Most Out of Your Practices

The way you do your exposure practices will have a big impact on the outcome. In this section, we describe some basic guidelines to keep in mind while practicing exposure, so you can maximize the likelihood of your fear decreasing with practice. Most of these recommendations are based on studies that have tested out the effects of practicing exposure in various ways (Antony and Barlow 2002). Other recommendations are based on years of clinical experience with our own clients.

PLAN YOUR PRACTICES IN ADVANCE

Decide beforehand what you will do and when you will do it. We recommend scheduling your exposure practices just as you would any other appointment. Ideally, this should be done at the beginning of each week or even further in advance. If you formally schedule your practices, you will be much more likely to follow through. You also may want to include other people in your practices. Making a commitment to another person to go to a high place may increase the likelihood of your going there.

TAKE STEPS AS SOON AS YOU FEEL READY

Nothing is more motivating than seeing quick changes. Trying more difficult exposures earlier in the process will lead to more fear and discomfort in the short term, but it will also lead to more rapid improvements. We recommend that you take steps as quickly as you are willing to. If you feel like you can try a more difficult item on your hierarchy despite your fear, then go for it. The worst thing that can happen is that you may feel very uncomfortable and will have to take a step back and try something easier.

AVOID NEGATIVE SURPRISES

There is evidence that exposure works best when it is predictable. You will get the most out of your treatment if you know what to expect. If you're with other people, it's important that they respect your need to avoid negative surprises; they should not purposely try to frighten you, for example, by pretending that they might jump off a ledge.

If you are afraid of unpredictable events, which do occur from time to time, they can be built into your exposures as later steps. If a bird flying by might trigger panic when you are standing on a fire escape, then you can simulate this situation as an exposure practice. You can have someone throw something, like a crumpled piece of paper, in front of your visual field while you stand in a high place. If you decide to introduce unpredictable events like this into your exposures, they should not be introduced until you are ready and have approved the plan to add the surprises. Also, under no circumstances should you introduce any variables that are dangerous. More on this later.

STAY IN THE SITUATION, DESPITE YOUR FEAR

One of the most important findings across studies on exposure-based treatments is that longer exposures are more effective than briefer exposures. How long is long enough? For years, experts have recommended that people stay in feared situations long enough for their fear to decrease. However, research suggests that even if your fear doesn't decrease during a particular practice, you will still likely benefit from the session (Craske and Mystkowski 2006). The key is to stay long enough to learn that your anxious predictions don't come true and that the situation is safer than you originally thought. In practice, exposure sessions should last at least thirty minutes and up to two hours. At our center, we typically schedule sessions for about ninety minutes. If the person's fear decreases sooner than that, we use the time to move on to a more difficult step on the hierarchy. In addition to these "official" practices, it is fine to take advantage of brief exposure opportunities as they arise throughout the week (such as driving over a bridge on your way to work).

PRACTICE FREQUENTLY

Another important guideline is to ensure that exposure practices occur very frequently and close together. Research has shown that exposure practices conducted once per day will lead to better outcomes than exposure practices conducted once per week, even when the total time spent doing exposures is equivalent (Foa et al. 1980). We recommend that you complete exposure practices at least three to five times each week until your fear has decreased significantly or at least during the first couple of weeks of your treatment.

PHASE OUT YOUR SAFETY BEHAVIORS

Safety behaviors are behaviors that you use to protect yourself from perceived danger or from unpleasant anxiety symptoms when you are in a place that makes you feel uncomfortable. In the case of height phobia, typical safety behaviors include the following:

- Not looking down when near a high ledge

- Making sure that you always have someone with you in high places, just in case

- Holding on to a wall or railing

- Avoiding getting too close to the edge

- Sitting down instead of standing

- Driving in the inside lane on bridges and elevated roads

- Distracting yourself from feelings of anxiety (like dizziness) by imagining being else-where, by listening to music, or by talking to someone else

When conducting exposure practices, it is important to reduce your reliance on these behaviors. Like avoidance, safety behaviors prevent you from learning that your feared situations are, in fact, not dangerous. As long as you are doing small things to protect yourself in high places, you may end up believing that your survival was due to these behaviors rather than to the fact that the situation itself is safe. Safety behaviors also prevent you from learning that, without behaving this way, you can tolerate the anxiety or distress that you experience in high places.

It may be difficult to eliminate your safety behaviors right at the start of your treatment. If so, it is perfectly fine to eliminate them gradually. For example, if you fear driving over bridges, you might begin your exposures by driving in an inside lane and then work up gradually to driving in the outside lane.

PRACTICE IN DIFFERENT SITUATIONS

It is best not to limit your practices to a single situation. If you fear riding on escalators, you will get more out of your treatment if you practice riding on several different escalators. Using one escalator would likely lead to your being less afraid on that particular escalator, but it might not lead to the same result on other escalators. Why? Different escalators have different features. Speed, height, steepness, openness (whether there are walls on both sides), lighting, and background noise can all vary from one escalator to the next. Chances are that your fear is affected by these variables even if you are unaware of it.

The same rule applies to other situations that you may fear. If you fear bridges, practice driving over several different bridges. If you fear balconies, practice being on different types of balconies. Practicing in a wide range of situations and locations will likely lead to a better outcome, especially over the long term.

DON'T FIGHT YOUR FEAR

When feeling uncomfortable, it is natural to want to make the feeling go away. Trying to control, fight, or avoid the experience of fear is not likely to work in the long run, however. In fact, attempts to control your fear can have the opposite effect over time. Fighting your fear will only serve to keep it there and may even make it worse. An alternative approach is to let the fear happen without trying to change it. Notice it, but don't evaluate it as negative, and don't try to fight it. Your feelings may be uncomfortable, but they are not dangerous, and they will eventually decrease on their own.

DON'T DO ANYTHING DANGEROUS

There is a famous photo from the 1930s of construction workers eating lunch while sitting on a crossbeam hundreds of feet above the ground during construction of the Empire State Building. Fortunately, getting over your fear of heights won't require you to do anything like this. A healthy respect for high places is actually a good thing in that it can protect you from real danger in certain situations.

Exposure practices should not include any situations that most people would view as dangerous. For example, standing right at the edge of a building's roof without a railing is probably not a good idea. Similarly, if you get dizzy in high places, it is probably best not to practice being near the edge of a high drop-off unless you have something to hold on to while your dizziness subsides. If you think a situation might be actually dangerous, but you're not sure, ask a few other people how they feel about it. If other people who don't fear heights view it as dangerous, chances are that it's a place where you don't need to be practicing.

Exposure to Feared Sensations

For many people, a fear of heights includes two components: a fear of high places and a fear of the sensations that they experience when in high places. For example, people who are afraid of standing on ladders may also fear experiencing feelings of dizziness on a ladder, because they believe that dizziness may lead to a loss of balance and falling.

Are there physical feelings that you fear when you are in a high place? Here are some of the physical sensations often associated with fear and anxiety: feeling dizzy, light-headed, or faint; trembling or shaking; racing and pounding heart; breathlessness or smothering sensations; sweating, hot flushes, or chills; numbness or tingling sensations; choking feelings; nausea; chest tightness or discomfort; blurred vision; feelings of unreality or depersonalization. Which, if any, of these sensations do you experience in high places? Are you frightened of any of these feelings, especially when you are in a high place?

If so, then exposure to the situations you fear will probably decrease your fear of these sensations. You can also practice bringing on these feelings directly, as part of your exposure hierarchy. If you fear experiencing dizziness while standing on a balcony, you might begin by practicing just being on a balcony, and when that gets easier, you can introduce practices in which you spin around for a minute before going on the balcony. Exposing yourself to feeling dizzy will help to decrease your fear of this feeling on the balcony.

Below are several exercises that you can use to bring on a variety of different sensations that people often fear (Antony et al. 2006). If these sensations don't scare you, there's no need to do these exercises. But if you are frightened of these feelings, especially in high places, you may find it useful to incorporate these exercises into your in vivo exposure practices.

Note: If you have a medical condition with symptoms that could be triggered or exacerbated by a particular exercise, you should not do the exercise without first checking with your doctor. For example, if you experience neck pain, don't shake your head; if you have asthma or if you have a cold, don't practice hyperventilation. Doing some of these exercises may result in unpleasant side effects even for individuals who are medically healthy. For example, spinning sometimes causes nausea and even vomiting, and hyperventilation sometimes triggers headaches. Again, use caution if you are concerned that an exercise may have effects other than triggering the harmless sensations you fear.

Exercises: How to Induce Feared Sensations

Exercise	Sensations
1. Spin in an office swivel chair for thirty seconds.	Dizziness, light-headedness, faintness, nausea
2. Shake head from side to side for thirty seconds.	Dizziness, light-headedness, faintness
3. Breathe through a small straw for three minutes (plug your nose if tempted to breathe through your nose).	Breathlessness, smothering sensations, racing or pounding heart
4. Hyperventilate for sixty seconds.	Breathlessness, smothering sensations, dizziness, light-headedness, faintness
5. Run in place for sixty seconds.	Racing or pounding heart, breathlessness, smothering sensations
6. Sit in a hot room or sauna for five minutes.	Sweating, hot flushes, breathlessness, smothering sensations
7. Stare at a spot on the wall for three minutes.	Feeling unreal or in a dream

An Alternative to Live Exposure: Virtual Reality

A number of studies have shown that virtual exposure to heights can be an effective alternative to live exposure (Emmelkamp et al. 2002). Virtual reality involves exposing yourself to a situation using a three-dimensional computer simulation. You wear a head-mounted display that includes a video screen to create visual images and stereo headphones to create the sounds associated with the situation. This technology can even be used to simulate the vibrations of an elevator, airplane, or other situations (by placing your chair on a platform fitted with vibrating devices). Because the images in VR are in three dimensions, the exposure feels more real than it might if you were just viewing the same images on a television screen. Also, the display covers most of your visual field, so the rest of the room you are sitting in is blocked out.

VR exposure doesn't work for everyone. However, for others it works well either on its own or as a step toward actual exposure. If you are interested in trying VR exposure, you will need to contact a therapist who delivers this treatment.

Two of the largest and best known clinics in the United States are the Atlanta Psychology Clinic, which is associated with Virtually Better (a company that produces and distributes VR software; www.virtuallybetter.com), and the Virtual Reality Medical Center, with three locations in California (www.vrphobia.com). The Virtually Better Web site includes a list of VR practitioners throughout the United States and in several other countries throughout the world.

How to Know When Treatment Is Finished

We recommend that you continue your exposures until you are able to enter the top situations on your hierarchy with minimal fear. The further you go in your treatment, the less likely your fear will be to return to a problematic level if you no longer continue to have a lot of exposure.

Of course, how far you go in your exposure practices is up to you. If you decide to end the treatment before reaching the top of your hierarchy, chances are that you will continue to experience some relief from your fear over the long term, though you may also continue to encounter some situations that are challenging.

Case Illustration: Alina's Fear of Open Heights

Alina was a twenty-eight-year-old accounting clerk who had been fearful of heights since she was a teenager or perhaps even earlier. She was unsure of how her fear had begun, but it seemed to be getting worse in recent years. Though she was comfortable standing in front of a window in a high building, sitting on an airplane, or riding in an elevator, she was terrified of being in high places that were open, even with a railing. Items on her exposure hierarchy included such activities as standing on a balcony, standing on a fire escape, walking down a large open staircase at a local shopping mall, standing near the railing on the second or third floor of the local mall, hiking and camping in elevated areas, skiing, driving over most bridges, walking over bridges and on elevated roads or sidewalks, and climbing a six-foot ladder to change a lightbulb.

Alina's boyfriend lived in a twelfth-floor apartment with a beautiful, large terrace that Alina found especially difficult. Overcoming her fear of being on the terrace was a high priority for her; summer was approaching, and her boyfriend was planning several parties on the terrace over the coming months. Depending on how close Alina was to the edge, being on the terrace ranged in difficulty from a moderate level (a rating of 50 out of 100 when she stood six or seven feet from the railing) to a high level (a rating of 90 when she stood right up against the railing).

Alina's first exposure began with standing on the terrace with her boyfriend. She decided to do the first practice at night, so she wouldn't be able to see how high she was. She also stood about seven feet from the edge of the terrace to avoid being able to see down. She felt better having her boyfriend with her, but she was nervous about having him stand too close, in case he bumped into her or pushed her closer to the edge. Therefore, she initially asked him to stand about four feet away from her. Over the next ten minutes, her fear decreased from a level of 50 to a level of 30, and she was feeling ready to move closer to the railing. She moved to a distance of four feet from the edge, and her fear shot up to a level of 75. She noticed that she felt drawn to the edge and imagined that she might lose control and jump off. Her boyfriend continued to stand a few feet from her, but he remained on the terrace to provide emotional support. After about five minutes, Alina's fear was beginning to come down again, and her concern about jumping off subsided. First, her fear decreased to 60, then to 50, and then to 30, all over a period of about thirty minutes. Alina was exhausted and decided to end the session. She planned to practice again the next day.

The next afternoon, she returned to the terrace, standing about four feet from the edge. Her boyfriend was with her. Her fear was high again (about 75 out of 100), because she could see much more clearly how high up she was. Over the next few minutes, her fear level increased to 90, and she decided to step back a bit. Now, at a distance of five feet from the edge, her fear was manageable—back to a level of 75. As her fear decreased, she gradually moved closer to the edge of the terrace. In ninety minutes, she was able to stand about a foot from the railing, with her boyfriend standing about a foot away from her, with her fear no higher than a level of 40.

Over the next week, Alina returned to the terrace twice more, about an hour each time. For each practice, she forced herself to eventually get right to the edge of the terrace and look down. She tried it with her boyfriend standing near her and with her boyfriend in his apartment, leaving her alone on the terrace. By the end of the week, she still felt a bit anxious while standing on the terrace, but only when she was alone, looking down over the railing. Even then, she was much more comfortable than she ever thought she would be. Alina felt ready to tackle another situation from her hierarchy.

She began with a trip to the mall, intending to practice standing by the railing on the third floor. When she got to the railing, she was pleasantly surprised to find that looking down was no longer scary. Her work on her boyfriend's terrace had helped her in this new situation. Rather than spending any more time at the third-floor railing, she decided to try the stairs. From the third floor, she began to walk down the stairs. Following her positive experience standing by the railing, she was disappointed to find that the stairs were more difficult than she'd expected them to be. There was something about being up high—being able to see all the way down while she was moving—that was more difficult than simply standing still near the railing. Her fear of walking down the stairs was at about 70 at the top of the staircase, and it decreased as she walked down. By the time she got to the second floor, her fear was minimal. Walking upstairs was easy as well. So, Alina decided to practice walking down the stairs from the third floor to the second floor, over and over again. After about an hour of practicing, she was able to do the walk with an anxiety level of only 25.

Alina was beginning to believe that she could overcome all of her height-related fears through exposure. Later the same week, she decided to try some new situations on her hierarchy. She figured she would tackle her fear of driving over bridges and elevated roads next. There was a particular bridge that she tended to avoid on the way to and from work. Driving over the bridge would cut ten minutes from her commute. Before practicing in rush hour, however, she practiced driving over the bridge for an hour on a Sunday morning, when there was little traffic. She began the practice as a passenger with her boyfriend driving and worked her way up so that she was the driver and her boyfriend was in the passenger seat. It took about twenty trips back and forth across the bridge for her fear to decrease from a level of about 80 to a level of 25. Over the next week, she practiced driving over the bridge each day, on her way to and from work. On three of the days, she took an extra fifteen minutes to drive over the bridge repeatedly. Her fear was higher the first time she tried it (after all, there was more traffic, and her boyfriend wasn't with her), but by the end of the week, driving over the bridge was easy, even in the outside lane.

Over the next couple of weeks, Alina drove over several local bridges, walked on an elevated road, and stood on a ladder, and none of these situations was particularly difficult. She was still nervous about skiing, but she wouldn't have the opportunity to try it for another few months, when winter arrived. She was also nervous about hiking in high places, but she was determined to try hiking later that summer. Even though she was still anxious in some high places, she knew that she had the tools to deal with her fear if she encountered a situation that made her feel panicky. Her fear had greatly decreased, and it no longer prevented her from doing the things she wanted to do.

Exercise: Expose Yourself to Your Feared Situations

Of all the exercises described in this book, this one is the most important. At this point, you have developed an exposure hierarchy and a treatment plan, and you have learned about the most effective ways to practice exposure.

Now you will put all of your planning into practice. In other words, it's time to begin your exposure sessions. Completing this exercise will take time, patience, and a willingness to feel uncomfortable temporarily in order to experience long-term relief from your fear of heights. Remember that your exposure sessions should be planned in advance and be structured, predictable, prolonged, and frequent. You should continue to practice in each feared situation until you are comfortable enough to move on to a more difficult item on your list.

Each time you complete a practice, record in your journal which steps you were able to complete (for example, standing five feet from the edge of a balcony for ten minutes, standing two feet from the edge for ten minutes, standing right at the edge and looking straight out for ten minutes, and standing at the edge and looking down for ten minutes). As you conduct each practice, record your fear level every five to ten minutes, using a scale ranging from 0 to 100, where 0 equals no fear at all and 100 equals as much fear as you can imagine.

Troubleshooting

Although exposure therapy is a very powerful strategy for overcoming fear, you may face some challenges during treatment. This section reviews these challenges and suggests ways to deal with them.

DEALING WITH OVERWHELMING FEAR

Sometimes, it's difficult to judge whether a particular practice is going to be too scary. In these cases, the decision to try a specific item on your hierarchy should be based on your best guess about whether you are ready. There is no harm in trying something difficult. The worst thing that will happen is that you will feel very uncomfortable. If you do find that your fear is overwhelming, take a short break for a few minutes and then try entering the situation again. Or, try something easier for a while, and then work your way back up to the difficult situation. For example, if you are standing on the tenth step of a fire escape and you are feeling too panicky to remain that high up, try moving down a couple of steps. After standing on the eighth step becomes easier, you can try climbing higher again. Overwhelming fear should not be a sign to give up completely. It's just a signal to perhaps try something a bit easier.

HANDLING AN UNPREDICTABLE EVENT

Out of thousands of people who have been referred to our center for phobia treatment over the years, no one has ever been hurt during an exposure practice. Of course, it is always possible that something could happen, and some of the people with whom we have worked have had unpleasant surprises. For example, one person with a driving phobia witnessed a minor car accident during a practice.

Similarly, a person with a snake phobia once had the pleasure of having a snake relieve itself on her.

If you plan exposures that are safe, chances are that you will not get hurt during your practices. However, small things may happen. Your foot may slip a bit while climbing a ladder. Or someone may accidentally bump into you while you are walking down a flight of stairs. These things happen to everyone from time to time. Early in your treatment, try to minimize the chances of the unexpected occurring (that is, don't practice on crowded stairs if you fear being bumped into). If you do have a negative experience that leads to your fear increasing, simply get back in the saddle and resume your exposure practices, even if it means temporarily moving back to an earlier step on your hierarchy. Later, you can purposely plan exposures that include unpredictable events (such as walking on crowded stairs and letting people bump into you).

FINDING THE TIME TO PRACTICE

One of the biggest challenges with exposure therapy is finding the time to practice. Often, when people have competing demands on their time, they will choose to do the easiest task, or the most urgent, or the one with the most immediate rewards. Unfortunately, exposure can be hard, there is no firm deadline, and the benefits are often not immediate. Not surprisingly, if you are forced to choose between practicing exposure and eating dinner, you will likely choose dinner. Although it can be difficult to find the time to practice, there are a number of strategies for increasing the likelihood that you will be able to complete your exposure practices:

1. As mentioned earlier, make sure that your exposures are written into your schedule like any other appointments.

2. Make a public commitment to practice your exposures. If you tell five people that you are planning to ride a Ferris wheel on the weekend, you may be more likely to do it than if you don't make a public declaration.

3. Recognize that some exposure is sometimes better than no exposure. If you don't have time to do as much exposure as we recommend, don't give up completely. Do what you can.

4. Build exposures into your everyday routine, so they don't have to take up extra time. For example, if you are planning to eat out one evening, choose a restaurant that's at the top of a hotel, and get a table with a view.

5. Remember that unlike some other difficult tasks (like staying fit and getting exercise), regular exposure need not be a lifelong commitment. A few short weeks of exposure will probably make a big dent in your fear, and the improvements will probably be long lasting.

6. Consider clearing your schedule to make time for your exposure practices. Take a couple of vacation days from work and spend them practicing exposure for a couple of hours in the morning and a couple of hours in the afternoon. Or hire a babysitter for a few evenings if you have children and need more time to practice.

COPING WITH FEAR STAYING HIGH

Sometimes fear doesn't decrease during a particular exposure practice. If your fear has not decreased during a practice, there are a few possible reasons:

1. Perhaps you have not stayed in the situation long enough. With some people, it can take an hour or two, or even longer, for their fear to come down. For brief situations (walking down a steep flight of stairs), prolonged exposure may mean repeating a brief practice over and over again.

2. Fighting your fear, engaging in safety behaviors, or focusing on how you might escape may prevent your fear from decreasing during exposure practices.

3. Life stress can affect your level of fear and whether it decreases during a particular exposure. If you have had a stressful day

at work, or if someone you care about is seriously ill, you may find that your fear of heights is greater and that it stays higher during your exposure practices. When your stress subsides, you will probably find your height phobia treatment getting back on track as well.

If none of these reasons can account for your fear not coming down, and you're still not experiencing any fear reduction during exposures, don't fret. You don't need to experience fear reduction during each session to experience improvement across several sessions. Even if your fear stays high during a particular practice, you may still benefit from exposure over the long term.

OVERCOMING FEARS OF REALISTICALLY DANGEROUS SITUATIONS

This book is designed to help you overcome fears of high places that most people would agree are not usually dangerous. However, you may need to do things that most people would see as dangerous: washing windows while standing on a scaffold on the side of a high building, standing at the edge of a high cliff, walking on an elevated beam at a construction site, or jumping out of an airplane with a parachute. For these sorts of situations, the principles of exposure may still work, though exposure-based strategies have not been studied for overcoming what many people would describe as realistic fears. If you need to feel more comfortable in these sorts of situations, and you are using exposure strategies to practice being in them, be sure to take adequate precautions to ensure your safety.

Summary

Exposure to high places is the only approach consistently found to be effective for overcoming height phobia. Although it is natural to want to avoid places that make you feel uncomfortable, avoidance helps to keep your fear alive. During exposure practices, your fear will initially increase, but with exposure, fear almost always decreases over time. For exposure to be effective, you should plan practices in advance, and your practices should be predictable and under your control. Your exposures also need to last a while, and they should occur at least three times per week. As you practice, you should try to prevent any unnecessary or excessive behaviors that you typically use to protect yourself in the situation. If you are frightened by particular physical sensations, such as dizziness, you can also practice bringing on these sensations when in high places. A number of challenges may arise during your exposure practices, and this chapter discusses some possible solutions.

6

Changing Your Thoughts

When you're in situations that you fear, you may have noticed that certain ideas or thoughts run through your head. Or when you know you have to cross a high bridge or enter some other scary situation, you may picture all sorts of bad things happening. This is another important aspect of your fear: the fearful thoughts, beliefs, and predictions you make about heights and what might happen in high places. Don't worry if you haven't noticed any fearful thoughts at this point; sometimes these thoughts are so quick and automatic that they may occur outside of your awareness. However, the way you think about a particular situation can have a huge impact on how scared you become.

Imagine the following scenario. Ellen has been invited for a drink with her friend on his twentieth-floor balcony to watch the sunset. Before heading for the balcony, Ellen notices herself worrying about different outcomes, such as getting dizzy and falling off the balcony, or the railing of the balcony coming loose, or the balcony crumbling beneath her. Not surprisingly, her fear starts to skyrocket and she decides to stay inside.

In a second scenario, imagine it's someone else named Jane who's invited for a drink on the balcony. Jane doesn't think about all those scary things that ran through Ellen's mind. In fact, when Jane's friend points out a loose part of the railing, Jane thinks to herself that the whole railing still looks pretty sturdy, so she'll just avoid leaning against the loose part. Jane is able to enjoy the sunset with her friend.

Why did Ellen and Jane have such different experiences? The situation was the same, an offer to sit on a high balcony with a friend. But whereas Ellen's mind was filled with fearful thoughts of bad things that could happen, Jane believed that the realistic danger to her was minimal. Given the differences in their thinking, it's no wonder that their levels of fear were also very different.

Ellen's style of thinking is common among people with anxiety problems. People with severe fears and anxiety disorders often have beliefs that are exaggerated or biased in terms of noticing or thinking about all the bad things that might happen. People with severe fears also tend to notice and remember information that is consistent with their fears. If both Ellen and Jane came across a news story about someone falling from a high place, who do you think would notice and remember that story better? If you guessed Ellen, you are probably right.

Although the exposure strategies that you learned in chapter 5 are the most effective way to get over your fear of heights, you may also benefit from challenging the negative thoughts and beliefs that contribute to your fears.

This chapter describes some *cognitive strategies* to help you figure out the types of fearful thoughts and beliefs you might have about heights and how to change these ideas. Though these techniques have not been studied specifically for the treatment of height phobia, they have been found to be useful for a wide variety of other anxiety-based problems (Barlow 2002).

Of course, some of our fearful thoughts about high places are realistic. It's true that actually falling off a tenth-story balcony would be terrible and dangerous. Sometimes fearful thoughts and worries actually serve a purpose in keeping you safe and on the lookout for real danger. On the other hand, the fearful thoughts associated with phobias tend to be exaggerated and out of proportion to reality. The strategies discussed in this chapter are appropriate for challenging these exaggerated and unrealistic fears.

Identifying Fearful Thoughts

Before you can challenge or change your fearful thoughts, you have to figure out what they are. Again, these thoughts are sometimes hard to notice because they occur so quickly and automatically. However, with some patience and attention, you should be able to figure out what kinds of fearful predictions you have about high places. These predictions may include thoughts about the situation itself (such as Ellen's fear of the balcony crumbling beneath her). They may also include thoughts about your own reactions to being in a high place (a fear of your legs getting shaky or rubbery). Here are some other examples of fearful thoughts that people with a height phobia often have:

- *I'll fall.*

- *I'll get pushed off the edge.*

- *I'll trip and fall as I climb down that hill.*

- *This machine will get stuck and I'll never get down.*

- *I'll die.*

- *I'll become injured and end up a vegetable.*

- *I'll get light-headed and faint.*

- *I'll get vertigo, and I couldn't stand those feelings.*

- *I might throw myself off a high place.*

- *I'll lose control, start screaming, and make a fool of myself.*

- *My fear will be obvious to others, and they'll think I'm an idiot.*

As a first step toward noticing your anxious thoughts, ask yourself what you're worried about when you have to go into a feared situation. Are you worried about something bad happening? If so, what in particular? Are you worried about embarrassing yourself or feeling uncomfortable? If so, how do you think that might happen?

If you still can't figure out your fearful thoughts and beliefs, you might have more success by putting yourself in an anxiety-provoking situation. It is often easier to notice fearful thoughts and predictions when you are actually in a scary situation. Perhaps pay attention to your thoughts when you are trying an exposure practice.

Exercise: Identify Your Fearful Thoughts

Think about all the situations to do with heights that scare you. For each situation, think about the reason for your fear. Are you worried about getting hurt? Dying? Are you worried about feeling certain physical sensations? Are you worried about doing something silly or embarrassing? Write down all the thoughts, worries, and predictions that come into your mind. Do any of the sample thoughts above fit your experience? If so, write those down as well.

Challenging Fearful Thoughts

Now that you have identified some of your fearful thoughts, you can begin to change them. The goal is not simply to replace your fearful thoughts with less fearful ones; it is, rather, to learn to think more realistically about the situations you fear. If you believe that it might be dangerous to stand close to the edge of a cliff with no railing, your belief may not be too far off the mark. We don't want to change a thought like this, because it serves a protective function;

it keeps you a safe distance from the edge of a cliff! On the other hand, if you think there's a 90 percent chance you will fall off a tall bridge when driving across it, it's likely that this thought doesn't reflect reality. It is this type of thought you want to change.

The first step toward changing these types of thoughts is to treat your fearful predictions as possibilities rather than facts. Once you allow yourself to consider that your fears may not necessarily reflect reality, you can take steps to discover how true your beliefs really are. Think of someone you know who is not afraid of heights, and ask yourself if he or she would agree with your fearful thoughts. Unless a fearful thought reflects a realistic danger, it is pretty unlikely that someone else would agree with it. You can also ask yourself these kinds of questions:

- Do you know for certain that something bad is going to happen to you?

- Have you had previous experiences in similar high places that have gone fine?

- Do other people do what you're about to try (such as climb a ladder to wash your windows) with no negative outcomes?

- What would your friends or family say about this situation?

- If you get nervous or panicky, can you handle that?

- Are you exaggerating the scary things that might happen?

In addition to asking yourself these types of questions, there are some specific strategies you can use to challenge your fears. These are described below.

EDUCATION

One of the most useful first steps you can take to challenge your fearful thoughts is to find out more about your feared situation. For example, some people who fear driving over bridges worry about the bridge collapsing. However, if you look at the statistics on bridges collapsing, you'll quickly realize that very few bridges around the world have collapsed over the past 150 years. Given the huge number of bridges found around the world, the number of collapsed bridges quickly becomes a tiny percentage. If you are someone who needs to climb ladders or work in high places, like roofs, educate yourself about reasonable safety precautions to take. Your local workplace safety organization likely has some tips or guidelines to ensure that you are as safe as possible while completing your job. If you follow these guidelines, your risk of being seriously hurt is minimized.

It's also helpful to consider that there is some risk associated with almost every activity. You could trip and fall when just walking on the sidewalk. Anyone who drives is vulnerable to being in a car accident. However, people don't usually avoid these kinds of activities, because the benefits are worth more than any small risks that these activities may present. It is probably worth it to you to continue driving, even though there is always a small chance you could be in an accident. Try to take this perspective when it comes to going into a high situation. For example, Peter (described in chapter 3) was afraid of going onto the observation deck of the CN Tower in Toronto. He was worried that he might fall over the edge of the deck or that the floor might collapse. So Peter used some cognitive strategies to question the realistic chance of these things happening. He educated himself by calling the CN Tower to ask a few questions about the history of the structure. He found out that in more than twenty-five years since the tower was built, no one had ever fallen off the deck and the floor had never collapsed. He also reminded himself that crossing the street to get to the tower was probably more dangerous than going up in the tower. By putting his fear in this perspective, he was able to see that the realistic risk to him was minimal.

We have a word of warning about educating yourself, however. Remember that the general public is often more interested in stories about disasters and accidents than about hearing of people who successfully climb ladders or stand on balconies. Therefore, if you look for information on the Internet or in the media, you will likely find scary stories about catastrophic events involving heights. A hiker falling over a cliff gets far more media coverage and attention than all those people taking successful and safe hikes every day. When you come across these types of stories, it is important to view them as exceptions, not the rule.

Exercise: Educate Yourself

Think about your feared situations. In your journal, make a list of some of the questions you have about entering these situations. Jot down any question you have about how to be safe in high places (such as how to safely use a ladder). Next, think of someone you can contact who can answer these questions. Do you have a friend or relative who is knowledgeable about your situation? Can you phone a city official to ask about city buildings or parks? Would the Internet be a good source of information? Contact the person or your source of choice to help you conclude whether or not you really need to be scared.

CHALLENGING EXAGGERATED THINKING

Many people with a fear of heights will assume the chance of something bad happening is very high, even when the realistic chance is quite low. This type of thinking error is sometimes called a *probability overestimation*. This thinking error is common; we all make probability overestimations from time to time. Nevertheless, this type of thinking can contribute to your fear and anxiety. Here are some examples of probability overestimations about heights:

- *The window will collapse if I lean against it.*

- *There is a 90 percent chance I will fall off this ladder.*

- *I will get vertigo while hiking, and I will fall over the edge of a cliff.*

- *I will go crazy if I have to go on the roof terrace.*

- *The Ferris wheel will break when I'm at the top.*

One of the most important ways to challenge a probability overestimation is to examine the evidence you have for the scary prediction actually coming true. In essence, this means taking all the information you have learned through talking to others and educating yourself, and combining it with all your previous experiences in the scary situation. If you find that you have had many experiences that support your belief, and so have others, perhaps your fears are realistic. On the other hand, if you find that your predictions generally have not come true in the past, perhaps your fears aren't realistic. If you find yourself making a scary prediction, you can ask yourself the following to determine if it is a probability overestimation:

- What have you learned from past experiences in this type of situation? Do you have evidence to suggest that your fears will come true? If so, were there also times when your feared consequences didn't happen?

- What have other people experienced in similar situations?

- What have you learned from educating yourself about the realistic chances of something bad happening?

- Are there ways this situation could turn out that are different from your scary predictions?

- What is the worst possible outcome? What is the best possible outcome? Realistically, what is the most likely outcome?

Let's look at how Marnie challenged her fear of the Ferris wheel breaking when she was at the top of the ride.

Fearful prediction: "The ride will break, and my compartment will collapse while I'm at the top of the Ferris wheel."

Evidence supporting her fears: "I've heard news stories of amusement park rides breaking down. I got stuck in a Ferris wheel once before. The rides at this fair are getting older. I heard of someone climbing down from a stuck compartment and falling on a Ferris wheel."

Evidence that doesn't support her fears: "I've been on lots of rides that didn't get stuck. The maintenance people at the fair assured me that the rides are checked on a regular basis for safety. The person who fell off the Ferris wheel had climbed out of the compartment. I would never try to climb down. Most of my friends have gone on lots of rides and never gotten stuck. According to one Web site from a law office specializing in accident claims (www .weitzlux.com), there were only two Ferris wheel–related injuries in the United States between 1987 and 2000."

Rational conclusion: "There is very little chance the ride will get stuck. There is no evidence that I will fall from the top of the Ferris wheel or get hurt. If the ride gets stuck, I can sit in my compartment and wait for them to fix it."

Let's look at another example of challenging probability overestimations. Jim is afraid of hiking on elevated trails.

Fearful prediction: "I will get vertigo or get dizzy, lose control, and fall over the edge of the hiking trail."

Evidence supporting his fears: "I've heard of people falling over when they get vertigo. I've been dizzy in high places lots of times."

Evidence that doesn't support his fears: "I've never actually had true vertigo. I've felt dizzy hundreds of times before and have never lost control or fallen over. I've even felt dizzy while hiking before, and nothing bad has ever happened."

Rational conclusion: "In reality, it's very unlikely that I will fall, even if I get dizzy."

Exercise: Examine the Evidence

Look at all the fearful thoughts that you've recorded in your journal. Try to pick out any probability overestimations. List any evidence in support of your fearful thoughts, as well as evidence against your fearful thoughts. Once you're done, try to summarize all the information in front of you into a rational statement about the actual risk in the situation. Be as realistic as possible. Ask yourself whether your conclusion would stand up in court if a judge were to look at all your pieces of evidence.

CHALLENGING CATASTROPHIC THINKING

Another common type of thinking error is *catastrophic thinking*, or *catastrophizing*, which is when you think that an outcome will be unbearable or horrible if it were to happen. Here are some examples:

- *If I have a panic attack on a balcony, I won't be able to cope.*

- *I'll freak out if I have to go over a bridge.*

- *Being frightened in front of my friends would be terrible.*

- *When I'm on the roof, I won't be able to manage being scared.*

Of course, sometimes people are afraid of negative outcomes that would be true catastrophes; that is, falling over a 100-foot ledge would be terrible. But there are lots of outcomes that seem like they might be terrible but would actually be manageable. To challenge catastrophic thinking, use the following questions:

- Realistically, what is the worst thing that might happen? (For example, you might feel very uncomfortable, get dizzy, have a panic attack.) If this were to occur, could you handle it?

- If other people were to notice you being uncomfortable, would they be sympathetic or cruel? In either case, does how they would react really matter?

- If you really embarrass yourself, how long would people actually think or talk about it?

- What would you say to a friend if they told you they had the same fears?

- Is it possible that things will turn out differently from your predictions?

- If your feared prediction actually happened, would it matter as much to you next week? Next year?

Here are some examples of how to challenge catastrophic thoughts:

Catastrophic thought: "I'll start to shake if I have to go on the balcony, and everyone will see that I'm scared and make fun of me. That would be a disaster!"

Rational response: "So what if I shake a bit when I'm on the balcony? I've seen my friends be scared in other situations. If they're truly my friends, they won't really care about it. They probably won't even talk about it later. They're more interested in their own lives."

Catastrophic thought: "If I panic when I'm on the bridge, it means that I'm back to square one."

Rational response: "I can handle panic attacks. I've had lots before and lived through all of them. I'd only be back at square one if I stopped trying to challenge my fears."

Exercise: Challenge Catastrophic Thoughts

Look over your list of fearful thoughts again. Do you notice any catastrophic thoughts? If so, try to come up with some rational responses using the questions above. Continue to notice and challenge catastrophic thoughts whenever they arise in your day-to-day life.

Troubleshooting

A number of difficulties can come up when you're trying to use cognitive therapy strategies to work on your fear. What follows is a discussion of some of the more common obstacles, along with some ideas of how to get around them. If you continue to have difficulty with these strategies even after finishing this chapter, however, don't worry. Exposure exercises are still the most effective way to challenge your fears. If you go through exposure without using any cognitive strategies, you will still likely have a great deal of success in overcoming your fear.

DIFFICULTY IDENTIFYING FEARFUL THOUGHTS

It's common for people to have trouble noticing or identifying their fearful thoughts. They are often referred to as *automatic thoughts* because they seem to occur automatically, with little conscious awareness. Also, your thoughts are not something you pay attention to on a regular basis, especially when you are in a scary situation. It's much easier to notice physical signs of fear, like a racing heart, dizziness, or sweaty palms, than fearful thoughts.

So, if you're having trouble noticing or identifying your fearful thoughts, try the following. First, right before you enter a scary situation or right after you get out of one, ask yourself what you're afraid of. Your thoughts might be easier to notice when your fear level is a bit higher, though not necessarily at its peak. Give yourself time to practice this new skill. With repeated effort, you might get better at noticing your thoughts, so they are less automatic and more accessible to your awareness. Use the examples provided in this chapter and throughout the book to see if they reflect your fears. You could also ask friends or family members for suggestions: what might they think or predict if they had the same fears as you? Also look for fear-provoking images. One person we worked with could not identify any fearful thoughts, but she noticed herself having images of swaying and falling over the edge when at a lookout in a park.

DIFFICULTY BELIEVING YOUR RATIONAL THOUGHTS

Sometimes when people come up with rational responses to their fearful predictions, it makes no difference to their levels of fear. In this case, they may realize that they have trouble believing in their own rational responses. One way to overcome a problem like this is to make sure you've really considered all the information or evidence about your fears. If you've ignored some information, your rational responses will seem empty. If you've been trying really hard to think positively, remember that the goal of the cognitive strategies is not to think positively but to think realistically. Make it your goal to come up with a rational response that does two things: it takes all the evidence about your fear into account, instead of just focusing on the worst-case scenarios, and it feels believable to you.

BAD EXPERIENCES WITH HEIGHTS

Another challenge that can come up when you're working on changing your thoughts is what to do if you've actually had a bad fall or known someone who was seriously or fatally injured after falling from a high place. In this case, you should try to remember that for every serious fall or injury, there have been numerous times that people have safely gone into high places. Considering all the information about a situation can help you decide whether it is truly dangerous and should be avoided.

Summary

This chapter introduced the idea that how you think about a situation can have a strong impact on how you feel about that situation. People with a height phobia often have scary thoughts or images about what will happen to them in high places and whether they can handle their fearful reactions. These thoughts or images are often unrealistic, with too much of a focus on the bad things that could happen and not enough focus on whether the situation is truly dangerous. This chapter talked about two types of thinking errors: probability overestimations (overestimating the likelihood of something bad happening) and catastrophic thinking (overestimating how bad something will be if it were to happen). It presented strategies for how to challenge these thinking errors to ensure that your predictions about high places are as realistic as possible. Changing your thoughts is a difficult skill to learn, and problems may arise along the way. The chapter closed with several strategies for overcoming common obstacles that can arise when using cognitive therapy strategies.

7

Staying Well

By now, you may have noticed significant changes in your level of fear in high places and your ability to tolerate high situations. As you continue to practice the exposure strategies from chapter 5 and the cognitive strategies from chapter 6, your fear should continue to decrease, ideally to where you have met all your treatment goals. Once you have reached that point, it is important to turn your attention to maintaining these gains. The aim of this chapter is to give you some strategies to maintain your progress over the long term.

What Can Make Your Fear Return?

A number of factors can contribute to a return of fear. However, keep in mind that most people maintain their improvements over time, and if fear returns, the level of fear is not the same as it was when you first started. If your fear returns, you will not be back to square one. In fact, if you're aware of the factors that may contribute to your fear, you will probably be able to handle the situation and manage the fear before it becomes overwhelming. Here are some factors that may lead to fear coming back.

ALLOWING AVOIDANCE BEHAVIOR TO RETURN

As you have learned, avoiding your feared situation maintains your fear. The more you avoid, the more your body may forget what you've learned about the relationship between high places and safety. Old associations between high places and fear can start to emerge again. Therefore, it is essential that you keep on the lookout for times when you avoid feared situations.

Avoidance can be obvious (not going on a hike with your friends; taking a driving route that steers clear of high bridges), but it can also be subtle. Examples of subtle avoidance include going up to a high floor of a building but never going near the window, taking antianxiety medications with you when you need to enter a feared situation, or turning up your stereo in the car to distract yourself when you have to drive over a high bridge or road. These forms of subtle avoidance may not seem like a big deal, but they can add up to a bigger problem over time.

Be on the lookout for any forms of avoidance in your life. Ask your family and friends to help you with this job. Ask them to point it out if they notice you starting to avoid situations. It will be much easier to tackle your avoidance if you notice it right away and work on changing it before it becomes an entrenched pattern.

NOT CONTINUING WITH EXPOSURES AFTER YOU HAVE REACHED YOUR GOALS

Make sure that you do periodic exposure exercises. You may have an urge to stop doing them. Exposures are time consuming and can be anxiety provoking. Once you have conquered your fear, they may seem unnecessary. However, continued exposures are essential if you want to keep your fear at bay.

Fortunately, you don't need to keep doing exposures with the same intensity and frequency as you did during treatment. If you have achieved your goals, you just need to make sure that exposures are a regular part of your life. With heights, you may find it easy to build exposures into your everyday life. If you work in an office building with a number of floors, you can make sure to visit a friend or colleague on a high floor on a regular basis. If you have returned to hiking, you can schedule regular hikes along challenging routes. If you have a fear of certain bridges, you can make sure your driving route involves those bridges.

If it's difficult to continue doing exposures on a regular basis, you'll have to be more creative. Remember Peter, who was afraid of going to the top of the CN Tower in Toronto? He couldn't incorporate that particular exposure into his everyday life, so he did other exposures regularly that were easy to fit into his schedule, including occasional visits to the top story of a twenty-five-story building near his workplace. He also routinely reminded himself of his CN Tower success, using his work computer to repeatedly play a slide show of pictures he took from the top of the tower. This way, Peter was able to have mini exposures on a daily basis that reminded him of how he conquered his previous fear.

NOT DOING ENOUGH TYPES OF EXPOSURES DURING TREATMENT

Some people focus most of their exposure practices during treatment on a few specific situations. This can be useful, especially when the fear is limited to these situations. On the other hand, if your fear is more generalized, but you only practice exposures in a few situations, you may be left with pockets of fear that you haven't tackled. If you have a fear of high bridges, but you did all your exposures on a local high bridge, you may react with fear when you try to cross a new bridge. Again, it is important to do exposures in a wide variety of situations where your fear occurs. If you notice that you still have these pockets of fear, you may need to continue with exposures, focusing on new and varied situations.

HAVING A TRAUMATIC EXPERIENCE

Your fear might return if you have a traumatic experience in a previously feared situation or in a new high situation. Joe, a roofer, successfully overcame his fear of heights, but then he had an accident in which he was on a roof in wet conditions, slipped, and nearly fell over the edge of the roof. Joe seriously twisted his ankle during his slide, and he was off work for six weeks recovering. By the time he tried to return to work, his fear had spiked again. If you are unlucky and have a bad experience in a feared situation, our best advice is to return to your exposures as soon as possible.

Also, use cognitive strategies to challenge your fearful thoughts. Joe's accident made him think that he would be at high risk for injuring himself if he returned to his job. However, after considering all the times he had been on a roof without slipping, plus all the coworkers he knew who had never had an accident, and then thinking about the poor conditions that caused his slip, he was able to recognize that being on a roof wasn't generally dangerous and that he should take extra safety precautions in poor weather conditions. Joe was able to gradually return to work after completing a short hierarchy of exposure exercises.

If you have had a traumatic experience, you may need to go back to your hierarchy or build a new one. If you do need to revisit old exposures, it may be quicker and easier to make progress the second time around because of your previous experience. This is especially true if you restart your exposures as soon as possible.

HAVING AN UNEXPECTED PHYSICAL REACTION IN A FEARED SITUATION

Fear can sometimes return if you have an unexpected and uncomfortable physical reaction in a previously feared situation. You may experience light-headedness, dizziness, vertigo, shortness of breath, or any other uncomfortable sensation. Jennifer had conquered her fear of going down the escalator at her local mall, but one day, she had a panic attack while riding this very escalator. She noticed her heart racing, she found it difficult to breathe, she began to tremble, and she thought she might faint.

Jennifer had experienced panic attacks in the past, but she hadn't had one on the escalator in months. The unexpected nature of her reaction caused her fear about the escalator to return. In the days following this panic attack, Jennifer noticed herself making excuses to avoid going to the mall, and she felt very scared about trying to use the escalator again.

It is understandable why some of Jennifer's fear began to return. Panic attacks are scary. But if your physical reactions to fear are uncomfortable, remind yourself that they are not dangerous. In fact, having some physical symptoms of fear while putting yourself in a previously scary situation should be expected! Even after you've conquered your fear, you will have odd or uncomfortable physical feelings from time to time. The human body creates lots of different sensations on a regular basis. You can also sometimes have more sensations than usual because of subtle environmental changes or because you haven't slept well, have had more coffee than usual, or watched an emotional movie.

The bottom line is to make sure you don't catastrophize the meaning of your physical sensations in a previously feared situation. Experiencing uncomfortable feelings doesn't mean that the situation has become dangerous or that you are back to square one. Continuing exposures is useful to prove to yourself that the situation has not become dangerous.

UNDERGOING LIFE STRESSES

Not surprisingly, increased life stress can cause a return of your fear. Life stress can take many forms, including both positive changes (getting married, moving, having a baby, starting a new job) and negative changes (losing your job, becoming ill, having family problems, experiencing the death of a loved one). Both forms of stress can lead to general feelings of anxiety, physical problems (such as headaches), low mood, edginess, and irritability. They can also affect your fear level in specific situations, including heights. By increasing your overall level of arousal, stress can make previously easy situations suddenly seem more difficult.

Learning to manage stress is a skill that most people can benefit from. Helpful strategies include taking a relaxation-based approach, such as yoga or slow breathing; doing more physical exercise; meditating; maintaining a well-balanced diet; talking to loved ones; and finding ways to solve the problems that contribute to your stress. Often, when the stress subsides, your fear of heights will decrease, provided that you haven't fallen into your old patterns of avoidance. With temporary stresses, the best thing to do is ride out the stress while continuing to expose yourself to your feared situations. If the stress in your life is chronic (such as ongoing stress at work), you may need to increase your exposures to balance out the impact of stress on your fear levels.

Making Sure Your Fear Does Not Return

Don't be discouraged after reading about how your fear may return. Remember, for most people the benefits of treatment last over the long term, and fear doesn't return to any significant level. This section describes some ways to make sure your fear doesn't return.

BE PREPARED

One of the most helpful things you can do is to be educated, aware, and prepared for the factors that might influence your fear. By reading this chapter thus far, you are already more prepared. Now that you know about the factors that can lead to fear returning, you can keep your eye out for them. We aren't suggesting that you constantly look for sources of stress—that would be exhausting. Rather, keep the above-mentioned factors in mind as you go about your day-to-day life.

Remember that pretty much everyone has difficult periods of high stress. What matters is how you cope: whether you decide to abandon the strategies you learned in this book or whether you plug away at exposures, even little ones, to keep your progress moving forward. Similarly, everyone has physical sensations in their bodies, and many of these sensations are hard to explain. What's important is not that you have feelings of panic; what's important is how you react to these feelings.

CATCH SYMPTOMS BEFORE THEY BECOME BIG PROBLEMS

It is much easier to fix a return of fear when it is still a small problem. If you pay attention to any symptoms of fear returning, you'll be better able to catch them before they escalate. Once again, however, we don't want you to spend all your waking hours being on the lookout for symptoms! Just make sure to pay attention if you sense little signs of your fear returning. If you notice yourself changing your driving route slightly to avoid a high bridge, standing farther away from the edge of balconies, or turning down invitations to do things that may involve heights, this might be a signal that your fear is starting to return, at least a bit. If you notice your physical reactions growing stronger in high situations, ask yourself if this symptom is due to something else ("I just had a coffee") or if it is a sign of increased fear.

MAKE A PLAN TO CHALLENGE
YOUR FEAR

If you sense your fear returning, make a plan to reconquer this fear before it becomes a bigger problem. Your plan might include rereading sections of this book to remind yourself of the information and strategies you learned. Other plans might be more active, involving more exposure exercises. You may need to take out your hierarchy and repeat some of your earlier exposures. Or if a return of fear involves a new situation, you may need to create a new hierarchy. Just try to remember that you have all the skills you will need to successfully challenge your fear of heights over the long term.

Consider the following example of a client who noticed a return in her fear levels and how she tackled this. Remember Alina from chapter 5? She successfully conquered her fear of heights, including high bridges, her boyfriend's terrace, and high staircases. She remained symptom-free for a number of months. Then, one day a coworker told her a story about how someone fell down five flights of stairs and broke his leg. Alina didn't initially have a strong reaction to this story, but over the next few weeks, she began to use some subtle avoidance and safety behaviors in high places. She began driving over bridges in the middle lane, instead of staying in the outside lane. She also began to take the elevator at the mall instead of walking up and down the open staircase.

Alina first noticed these symptoms when her boyfriend pointed them out. She quickly realized that she was doing these things because her fear had increased, and she made the connection with the story at work. She initially felt demoralized. However, after rereading some educational material, she remembered that a return of some fear is normal after a difficult experience. Alina decided to make a plan to get back on track. Her plan included the following:

- Eliminate safety behaviors like driving in the middle lane. Alina forced herself to use the outside lane when driving across all local bridges.

- Challenge fearful thoughts and predictions. Alina caught herself beginning to overestimate the likelihood that she would fall from a high place and seriously hurt herself. Instead of accepting this thought, she began to challenge it, focusing on all the times she had climbed stairs without being hurt and all the other people who successfully climb stairs every day.

- Schedule planned exposures for a few weeks. Alina wrote a new hierarchy with five exposure items. She began to practice exposures twice a week, for about an hour each time, until the five situations ceased to bother her anymore.

- Increase the opportunity for experiencing exposures in daily life. Alina took every opportunity that arose to challenge herself in day-to-day situations. For example, she volunteered to pick up a visiting relative from the airport, knowing that there were two bridges she would need to cross on the way.

By noticing her symptoms early and putting a plan into place, Alina was able to prevent a significant return of her fear. After a few weeks, she began to feel more comfortable in high situations again and was not avoiding anything.

Summary

The techniques described in this book are very effective at helping people with their fear of heights. But what happens once you're better? In most cases, people maintain their gains, but there is a chance that your fear will return in some form. This chapter reviewed the factors that may contribute to a return of fear. Suggestions for preventing your fear from returning include being educated about the factors that affect fear, learning strategies for managing stress, catching symptoms before they become big problems, and making a plan to deal with any fear that returns. A key point in staying well is to maintain exposures as a part of your life, especially during times when fear begins to grow.

8

Helping Someone Else with a Height Phobia

I f you are reading this chapter, then either someone with a height phobia has asked you for help or you are trying to figure out ways to help someone you know (perhaps a friend, child, or another family member) who wants to get over a fear of heights. Either way, this chapter will give you some suggestions for what you should and should not do to help someone who is fearful of heights.

Your role as helper is very important. Many people need a supportive coach, or helper, while they attempt to do some of the exercises that are necessary to overcome their fears. Also, though you may be trying to help, friends and loved ones of people with strong fears sometimes unintentionally do things that actually have the opposite effect in the long term. So your role as a helper may require changing some of your behaviors in a significant way. This chapter will first review some of the helpful things you can do for someone with a fear of heights. Then it will specifically address how to help a child who is afraid of heights.

Understand the Treatment

As a first step when helping someone with a fear of heights, you need to learn more about the recommended strategies for overcoming such fears. If your loved one is in treatment with a professional therapist, see if you can attend one or more sessions to get a sense of what strategies are being used. If you are going to coach someone who is not in therapy, we recommend that you read this entire book. If you don't have time for that, try to read some key chapters, including chapter 5, on exposure therapy. Exposure therapy is the most important strategy your loved one can use to overcome a fear of heights. Become familiar with all the guidelines for conducting exposure practices, such as making sure that practices are prolonged, repeated frequently, and under the fearful person's control. The more you understand the treatment techniques, the easier it will be to help your loved one use the strategies properly and stick with them.

Make Sure You Are Comfortable with Heights

To be an effective helper, you need to be comfortable being in a variety of high places. In other words, you need to be able to model a reasonable reaction in a high place and an ability to cope with any nervous feelings that come up. We don't expect a helper to never have nervous feelings in a high place. That would be unrealistic. However, helpers have to be able to calmly enter high situations and model an ability to stay in these situations, even if doing so is a bit scary. It wouldn't be much help to your loved one if you were to stand by the edge of a lookout and start screaming with panic! It's okay to acknowledge that looking over a cliff can make someone feel dizzy or that being up on a ladder is a bit anxiety provoking. Your willingness to do these things, despite a bit of anxiety, and to maintain your calm throughout will help teach your loved one a more appropriate reaction to the feared situation.

If you are not comfortable with heights and don't think you can model a calm reaction to a high situation, perhaps you should not be your loved one's helper. It may be better for him or her to find another helper who doesn't have this kind of fear.

Be Supportive and Empathic

It can be easy to forget how scary certain situations are for someone with a height phobia, especially if heights don't bother you. Some helpers have to fight the urge to blurt out, "Just get over it!" or "Don't be so silly."

It may be especially difficult to be supportive if your life has been adversely affected by your loved one's fears.

We have met many family members and friends who haven't been able to go on some vacations or who can't enjoy certain recreational activities with their loved ones due to their loved one's fear of heights. But even if there are good reasons to feel frustrated, it is very important to put aside those frustrations when helping your loved one. To maximize empathy, it can be useful to think about the most frightened you have ever felt in your life, and then remember that this is similar to how your loved one feels when in a high place.

Also remember that getting over a phobia takes a lot of hard work, and there may be twists and turns in the road. Be encouraging when your loved one has a tough day. Be excited when he or she takes a step forward. If you are going to accompany your loved one on exposures, be ready with words of encouragement and support to help him or her get through tough patches or hard exercises. Here are some examples of supportive things you can say to your loved one.

- "Stick with it."

- "Your fear will peak and then pass."

- "This is short-term pain for long-term gain."

- "You can do it. You're doing great."

- "This exposure will be worth it in the long run."

Offer No Surprises

A cardinal rule in helping someone with exposure practices is to offer no surprises. Your loved one should have complete control over each exposure practice, including what he or she chooses to do, how fast he or she takes things, and whether to alter the practice in some way to make it more difficult. Of course, there are factors that are outside of your control (such as whether a bird flies by during an exposure on a ladder). Your loved one should be in charge of all the factors that are controllable.

Here is an example of what not to do. Jeff was helping his wife Sabrina with her fear of heights. He knew that she'd been working on looking out of windows from the upper floors of her office building. To celebrate her progress, he decided to take her for a surprise dinner at a revolving restaurant at the top of a downtown high-rise. When Sabrina arrived at the building, she realized it might be too difficult for her. She attempted going up, but she felt panicked and dizzy as soon as she stepped off the elevator. The restaurant was at least ten stories higher than any practices she had completed, and it had floor-to-ceiling windows. Sabrina and Jeff ended up going home, much to both of their disappointments.

Although Jeff's intentions were good, this was a surprise exposure for Sabrina. It would have been better for him to discuss his plans with Sabrina up front, to see if she felt ready to try this. If she felt she wasn't ready, they could have made this dinner a goal to work toward, rather than something to try that night.

Avoid surprises during exposures, as well. It is not helpful to physically nudge or move your loved one closer to the edge of a high place, to make sudden movements (if moving objects are part of his or her fear), to pretend to do anything dangerous in a high place (such as only using one hand when climbing a ladder), or to drive across a scarier bridge than your loved one has agreed to go across.

Help Challenge Fearful Thoughts and Predictions

When people are in situations that scare them, they often experience anxiety-provoking thoughts or predictions. In fact, these thoughts and predictions help determine whether they will be scared (see chapter 6). Chances are that your loved one is thinking about scary consequences, such as falling, dying, or looking foolish. Other frightening predictions may include worries about structures collapsing or crumbling. In your role as helper, you can assist your loved one in both figuring out what his or her fearful thoughts are and helping to challenge these thoughts. Some useful questions for identifying fearful thoughts include the following:

- "What is your biggest fear right now?"

- "What are you afraid is going to happen?"

- "Do you have any scary images or memories in your mind right now?"

Once you and your loved one have a good idea of some of the fearful thoughts he or she is having, you can also play a role in helping to challenge these thoughts. Here are some helpful questions to ask your loved one:

- "Has your feared consequence ever happened?"

- "Have you been in a situation like this where nothing bad actually happened?"

- "What's your evidence that something bad will happen?"

- "What's the most likely thing that will happen?"

- "If you feel anxious or have a panic attack, can you live through it?"

- "If you feel embarrassed, how long will those feelings last?"

When helping to challenge your loved one's fearful thoughts, avoid getting into debates or arguments about how dangerous a situation is. If your discussion feels like it's becoming heated, perhaps stop this line of questioning and return to encouraging your loved one to complete the exposure. Also remember that it's important to be realistic about a feared situation, not simply to think positively. It's probably not a good idea to continually dismiss any real risk or bad experiences your loved one has had (such as a previous fall from a ladder). On the other hand, it is helpful to remind your loved one about all the times he or she has successfully climbed a ladder without incident.

Be Reliable

When you commit to helping a loved one work on his or her fear, it's important to be available and reliable with your help. For exposure exercises to be maximally helpful, a person needs to practice multiple times per week, for up to several hours per practice. If you cannot commit to being available for at least some of these practices, perhaps you are not the right helper. In addition, if you commit to helping with a practice, stick with it. We know that life happens, and things come up on a regular basis that can interfere with exposure practices. It is almost too easy to always find something else that seems more urgent than an exposure practice. Remember that your loved one will be struggling with the same issues, and he or she has the added stress of being the one who has to do the exposures! If you are unreliable or unavailable, this might give him or her the perfect excuse to avoid practicing.

Know When to Ease Out of Practices

Having a supportive coach to help with exposures is useful when initially trying to get over a fear. At some point, however, your loved one needs to be able to handle going into high places alone. So, another aspect of your job is to start to ease yourself out of exposure practices when your loved one starts to make significant progress.

This step is something that should be discussed both at the beginning of treatment and periodically throughout the program. You may need to ask your loved one whether he or she truly still needs you along, or whether your presence during practices is a safety behavior that should be gradually eliminated. If he or she is fearful of completing practices without you present, it may be useful to include some practices that gradually decrease your involvement in the exposures. Here are some examples of how to do this:

- Sitting in the backseat of the car, instead of the front seat, when driving over bridges

- Driving in another car behind your loved one when driving over bridges

- Standing a few feet back from your loved one in a high place

- Riding the next car on a Ferris wheel or other amusement park ride

- Being in the next room when your loved one climbs a stepladder

- Using walkie-talkies with your loved one on a hike, so you are within a reasonable distance but out of view

Be Prepared for Setbacks

There are twists and turns on the pathway to success. Difficult days, difficult exposures, and minor setbacks can be the norm. If you are helping someone overcome a height phobia, it's important for you to be prepared for difficulties if they arise. Don't be discouraged. Minor setbacks don't mean that treatment isn't working. As long as things are generally going in the right direction, you are on the right path. Be encouraging toward your loved one if he or she hits a snag or takes a step backward in progress. Brainstorm how to manage the snag. Sometimes the answer is as simple as chalking it up to a bad day and starting again tomorrow. At other times, it may be a bit more complicated than that and may require your loved one trying an easier exposure or going back to reread relevant chapters in this book. The most helpful thing you can do is make sure your loved one doesn't give up.

What You Shouldn't Do

We have tried to emphasize the helpful things you can do during your loved one's work toward conquering his or her fear. Here is a list of some don'ts—things not to do during treatment.

- Don't be pushy. You can be encouraging without pushing your loved one too hard. Remember that exposure should be at your loved one's pace, not your pace.

- Don't get frustrated with your loved one. Remember that exposure practices are very scary for people, which may lead them to act in difficult ways. In the long run, successful treatment will eliminate these difficult behaviors.

- Don't force your loved one to try something that is too difficult. Don't push him or her to stay in a situation if he or she cannot. Instead, encourage him or her to return to the situation as soon as possible, or to try a slightly easier exposure.

- Don't freak out in a high place. Try to model coping behaviors, not panicky behaviors.

- Don't talk about your loved one's treatment with others unless you have permission to do so. Respect your loved one's wishes to keep this work private.

- Don't tell your loved one that a particular situation is not dangerous. Instead, encourage him or her to tell you why the situation isn't dangerous. If your loved one can voice the reasons and arguments for why something is safe, he or she will find doing so more meaningful than being told the same things by you.

- Don't hesitate to educate yourself as much as possible about phobias and fears.

Working with Children

If you are a parent whose child is afraid of heights, most of the tips in this chapter are also relevant for you. Here are a few other issues more specifically relevant to a child's fear. First, you will need to ask yourself if your child's fear is normal and will pass as he or she grows older. This will have implications for whether you seek treatment or engage in a treatment program like the one described in this book.

Many childhood fears come and go across development. For example, most children are afraid of the dark at some point during their development but eventually grow out of this fear. It is possible that your child's fear of heights is also a transient fear that will naturally decrease over time. Our advice would be to consider how intense and pervasive your child's fear is. If the fear involves just a few situations that rarely come up, perhaps you don't need to worry too much about conquering this fear and can take a more wait-and-see attitude. On the other hand, if your child's fear comes up frequently and is beginning to interfere in his or her life, then perhaps a program like this is necessary. For example, Amelia's mother brought her for treatment when eight-year-old Amelia's fear of heights got to the point that she couldn't sleep on her bed for fear of falling off. Amelia began to sleep on her bedroom floor instead. Her mother also reported that Amelia was starting to complain of feeling sick before school, which seemed to be tied to Amelia's fear of her third-floor classroom.

Obviously, this fear was starting to have significant effects on Amelia's life, and her mother wanted to manage it before Amelia began to refuse going to school.

Another consideration when working with children is the important role that parents and loved ones can play in modeling appropriate reactions in high places. Children aren't born with the skills to know how to cope in stressful situations. Therefore, it is very useful for them to see and hear how others can cope in scary situations. Don't pretend that heights aren't a big deal; instead, talk out loud when in a difficult situation about how to get through it. Most of all, try to model exposure, not avoidance. Seeing anxiety in their parents can make it more difficult for children to overcome their own anxiety.

One difference between adults and children who have phobias is that children may not be particularly motivated to overcome their fear. Rather, they may just want to avoid the situation, regardless of the impact upon their life and the lives of their family members. If you have a child who needs to complete exposure practices, consider setting up a system of rewards for nonfearful behaviors and efforts. This can be as simple as using gold stars or heaping on the praise when your child tries something difficult. Or you can use more valuable rewards such as toys, books, or money. Remember to praise or reward completed practices, regardless of how your child feels during the practice. Your child will likely feel very scared when in a difficult situation, but the most important thing is whether he or she sticks it out.

Summary

This chapter reviewed some ways that loved ones can help someone conquer a fear of heights. The more educated, patient, and supportive you are as a helper, the better. It is also crucial to be encouraging, to not be pushy, and to never pull surprises during exposure practices. Although helpers can play an integral role in treatment efforts, at some point, they should ease themselves out of practices. This chapter provides some suggestions on how to gradually do this. It also provides a list of don'ts (what not to do if you are a helper). Finally, the chapter closes with some suggestions for helping a child with a fear of heights.

References

American Psychiatric Association. 2000. *Diagnostic and Statistical Manual of Mental Disorders*. 4th ed. Text revision. Washington, DC: American Psychiatric Association.

Antony, M. M., and D. H. Barlow. 2002. Specific phobias. In *Anxiety and Its Disorders: The Nature and Treatment of Anxiety and Panic*, 2nd ed., edited by D. H. Barlow. New York: Guilford Press.

Antony, M. M., T. A. Brown, and D. H. Barlow. 1997. Heterogeneity among specific phobia types in DSM-IV. *Behaviour Research and Therapy* 35:1089–1100.

Antony, M. M., D. R. Ledley, A. Liss, and R. P. Swinson. 2006. Responses to symptom induction exercises in panic disorder. *Behaviour Research and Therapy* 44:85–98.

Baker, B. L., D. C. Cohen, and J. T. Saunders. 1973. Self-directed desensitization for acrophobia. *Behaviour Research and Therapy* 11:79–89.

Barlow, D. H. 2002. *Anxiety and Its Disorders: The Nature and Treatment of Anxiety and Panic.* 2nd ed. New York: Guilford Press.

Biederman, J., J. F. Rosenbaum, D. R. Hirshfeld, S. V. Faraone, E. A. Bolduc, M. Gersten, S. R. Meminger, J. Kagan, N. Snidman, and J. S. Reznick. 1990. Psychiatric correlates of behavioral inhibition in young children of parents with and without psychiatric disorders. *Archives of General Psychiatry* 47:21–26.

Cook, M., and S. Mineka. 1989. Observational coding of fear to fear-relevant versus fear-irrelevant stimuli in rhesus monkeys. *Journal of Abnormal Psychology* 98:448–459.

Craske, M. G., and J. L. Mystkowski. 2006. Exposure therapy and extinction: Clinical studies. In *Fear and Learning: From Basic Processes to Clinical Implications*, edited by M. G. Craske, D. Hermans, and D. Vansteenwegen. Washington, DC: American Psychological Association.

Curtis, G. C., W. J. Magee, W. W. Eaton, H. U. Wittchen, and R. C. Kessler. 1998. Specific fears and phobias: Epidemiology and classification. *British Journal of Psychiatry* 173:212–217.

Emmelkamp, P. M., and M. Felten. 1985. The process of exposure in vivo: Cognitive and physiological changes during treatment of acrophobia. *Behaviour Research and Therapy* 23:219–223.

Emmelkamp, P. M., M. Krijn, A. M. Hulsbosch, S. de Vries, M. J. Schuemie, and C. A. van der Mast. 2002. Virtual reality treatment versus exposure in vivo: A comparative evaluation in acrophobia. *Behaviour Research and Therapy* 40:509–516.

Emmelkamp, P. M. G., and H. Wessels. 1975. Flooding in imagination vs. flooding in vivo: A comparison with agoraphobics. *Behaviour Research and Therapy* 13:7–15.

Foa, E. B., J. S. Jameson, R. M. Turner, and L. L. Payne. 1980. Massed vs. spaced exposure sessions in the treatment of agoraphobia. *Behaviour Research and Therapy* 18:333–338.

Fredrikson, M., P. Annas, H. Fischer, and G. Wik. 1996. Gender and age differences in the prevalence of specific fears and phobias. *Behaviour Research and Therapy* 26:241–244.

Gibson, E. J., and R. D. Walk. 1960. The "visual cliff." *Scientific American* 202:67–71.

Kendler, K. S., J. Myers, C. A. Prescott, and M. C. Neale. 2001. The genetic epidemiology of irrational fears and phobias in men. *Archives of General Psychiatry* 58:257–265.

Kirkpatrick, D. R. 1984. Age, gender, and patterns of common intense fears among adults. *Behaviour Research and Therapy* 22:141–150.

Lang, A. J., and M. G. Craske. 2000. Manipulations of exposure-based therapy to reduce return of fear: A replication. *Behaviour Research and Therapy* 38:1–12.

Menzies, R. G., and J. C. Clarke. 1993. The etiology of fear of heights and its relationship to severity and individual response patterns. *Behaviour Research and Therapy* 31:355–365.

———. 1995. The etiology of phobias: A non-associative account. *Clinical Psychology Review* 15:23–48.

Merckelbach, H., A. Arntz, W. A. Arrindell, and P. J. de Jong. 1992. Pathways to spider phobia. *Behaviour Research and Therapy* 30:543–546.

Mowrer, O. H. 1939. Stimulus response theory of anxiety. *Psychological Review* 46:553–565.

———. 1960. *Learning Theory and Behavior.* New York: Wiley.

Pendleton, M. G., and R. L. Higgins. 1983. A comparison of negative practice and systematic desensitization in the treatment of acrophobia. *Journal of Behavior Therapy and Experimental Psychiatry* 14: 317–323.

Pierce, K. A., and D. R. Kirkpatrick. 1992. Do men lie on fear surveys? *Behaviour Research and Therapy* 30:415–418.

Poulton, R., and R. G. Menzies. 2002. Non-associative fear acquisition: A review of the evidence from retrospective and longitudinal research. *Behaviour Research and Therapy* 40:127–149.

Rachman, S. 1977. The conditioning theory of fear-acquisition: A critical examination. *Behaviour Research and Therapy* 15:375–387.

Rapee, R. M., T. A. Brown, M. M. Antony, and D. H. Barlow. 1992. Response to hyperventilation and inhalation of 5.5 percent carbon dioxide-enriched air across the DSM-III-R anxiety disorders. *Journal of Abnormal Psychology* 101:538–552.

Seligman, M. E. P. 1971. Phobias and preparedness. *Behavior Therapy* 2:307–320.

Skre, I., S. Onstad, S. Torgersen, S. Lygren, and E. Kringlen. 2000. The heritability of common phobic fear: A twin study of a clinical sample. *Journal of Anxiety Disorders* 14:549–562.

Williams, S. L., S. M. Turner, and D. F. Peer. 1985. Guided mastery and performance desensitization treatment for severe acrophobia. *Journal of Consulting and Clinical Psychology* 53:237–247.

Martin M. Antony, Ph.D., is professor of psychology at Ryerson University in Toronto, ON. He is also director of research at the Anxiety Treatment and Research Centre at St. Joseph's Healthcare in Hamilton, ON. He has published twenty-one books and more than 100 scientific papers and book chapters in the areas of cognitive behavior therapy and anxiety disorders. He has received early career awards from the Society of Clinical Psychology (American Psychological Association), the Canadian Psychological Association, and the Anxiety Disorders Association of America, and is a fellow of the American and Canadian Psychological Associations. He is past president of the Anxiety Disorders Special Interest Group of the Association for Advancement of Behavior Therapy (AABT, now Association for Behavioral and Cognitive Therapies) and has been program chair for the AABT annual convention. He is actively involved in clinical research in the area of anxiety disorders, teaching, and education, and maintains a clinical practice. (www.martin antony.com)

Karen Rowa, Ph.D., is a psychologist at the Anxiety Treatment and Research Centre at St. Joseph's Healthcare and assistant professor in the Department of Psychiatry and Behavioural Neurosciences, McMaster University in Hamilton, ON. She received her Ph.D. in clinical psychology from the University of Waterloo and completed her predoctoral training at the Centre for Addiction and Mental Health in Toronto, ON. She completed a postdoctoral fellowship at the Anxiety Treatment and Research Centre before joining the faculty. Her research interests involve understanding ways to improve treatment outcomes for anxiety disorders. She has published numerous scientific papers and book chapters on the anxiety disorders and related topics. She is actively involved in clinical research, practice, teaching, and education.

more **simple solutions** to fear & anxiety
from new**harbinger**publications